AF479840

DR. SYREETA S. BOND DBA, PMP

International Project Strategies to Reduce the Negative Impact of Triple Constraints

Dedication

I dedicate this study to project managers who work on global projects. These global project managers are a rare breed of project managers who deal with the most complex projects in the world. I share your passion and your drive. Thank you for continuing to make the world better. I also dedicate this study to my daughter Estefani Sahara Bond. I was pregnant with her during my last year of study and held her in my arms throughout writing Section 3. She kept me motivated and busy.

Contents

Acknowledgement

I would like to thank the Most High for providing me with the resources and patience to fulfill my goal to complete my doctoral degree. I would like to thank my chair, Dr. Kenneth Gossett, for your support and guidance. I would like to thank my second committee member, Dr. Theresa Neal, for her support, guidance, and kind words throughout my study journey. I would also like to thank my URR reviewer, Jamiel Vadell, for all your support and for pushing me for greatness. My heartfelt thanks to my husband for keeping me motivated to finish. I would not have finished without you.

International Development Project Strategies to Reduce the Negative Impact of Triple Constraints

by

Syreeta S. Bond

DBA, Walden University, 2022
MBA, Keller Graduate School of Management, 2016
BA, Art Institute of Atlanta, 2013

Doctoral Study Submitted in Partial Fulfillment
of the Requirements for the Degree of
Doctor of Business Administration

Walden University
July 2022

Walden University

College of Management and Human Potential

This is to certify that the doctoral study by

Syreeta S. Bond

has been found to be complete and satisfactory in all respects,
and that any and all revisions required by
the review committee have been made.

Review Committee
Dr. Kenneth Gossett, Committee Chairperson, Doctor of
Business Administration Faculty
Dr. Theresa Neal, Committee Member, Doctor of Business
Administration Faculty

Dr. Jamiel Vadell, University Reviewer, Doctor of Business
Administration Faculty

Chief Academic Officer and Provost
Sue Subocz, Ph.D.

Abstract

With the growing number of international development projects not meeting the triple constraint requirements every year, organizational leaders exceed their budgets and increase schedule delays. Some project managers lack strategies to minimize the negative impact of these constraints, resulting in projects that exceed their budgets and have more delays. Grounded in the theory of constraints, the purpose of this qualitative multiple-case study was to explore strategies project managers use to reduce the negative impact of the triple constraints of cost, schedule, and scope on international development projects. The participants were five project managers from five different global development companies. Data sources included semistructured interviews with participants and research articles from the Project Management Institute knowledge database. The collected data were analyzed using a five-step thematic analysis process. Three themes emerged—(a) scope management, (b) stakeholder management, and (c) project management planning—yielded six strategies for managing international development projects. The key recommendations for project managers are to manage the project scope properly, communicate with key stakeholders, and adequately plan the project and its transition. Implications for positive social change include improving project management industry practices, adapting to cultural differences, increasing business profitability, and creating a safer work environment.

I

Part One

Foundation of the Study

1

Background of the Problem

As part of their work, international development project managers must negotiate cost overruns, schedule delays, and scope changes (Yap et al., 2017). Cost, schedule, and scope, otherwise known as the triple constraints, are the most critical elements of an international development project and often cause project failure. For example, 55% of Malaysia's construction projects were 80% or more higher in final price than initial cost estimates in 2017 (Yap et al., 2017). Similarly, 46% of Middle Eastern infrastructure projects experienced schedule delays, with only 36% of its projects completed within budget, in 2015 (Isharyanto et al., 2015). Negative impacts associated with the triple constraints of cost, schedule, and scope can lead to even more drastic results, such as the $16 Million PlayPump project in Africa, which bankrupted the charitable organization behind the project (Donnelly & Ika, 2017).

Due to the complexity, importance, and specificities of international development projects, further research is necessary to improve business strategy (Carral et al., 2018; Corti et al., 2017; Golini et al., 2018). Project managers worldwide continue to implement various strategies to reduce the negative impact on the triple constraints as much as possible; however, international development projects still fail at alarming rates. Researchers have found that conventional project management methodologies, processes, and tools are not feasible in every industry, especially international development projects (Mishra, 2016). They have concluded that further development of thinking processes and project management strategies are vital to project success and management projects. Therefore, project managers need strategies in international development projects to ensure project success leading to business prosperity.

2

Problem and Purpose

L eaders of international development projects struggle with several problems leading to a significantly high project failure rate (Mishra, 2016). As of 2017, 64% of donor-funded projects failed to achieve their intended impact due to poor project planning and management skills combined with organization-based structural and institutional problems (Corti et al., 2017; Golini et al., 2018; Kamu & Paul, 2018). The general business problem is that project managers in international development projects are negatively affected by cost, schedule, and scope, which results in loss of profitability for the business. The specific business problem is that some project managers handling international development projects lack strategies to meet the planned cost, schedule, and scope.

The purpose of this qualitative multiple case study was to explore the strategies project managers use in an international development project to reduce the negative impact of the triple constraints of cost, schedule, and scope. The target population comprised five project managers working at five international development project companies within the United Arab

Emirates (UAE) who have implemented successful strategies to meet projects' triple constraints of cost, schedule, and scope. The implications for positive social change include the opportunity to increase business profitability; increase wages for project managers; advance employment; and contribute to a healthier and safer environment for workers, workers' families, and their respective communities.

Population and Sampling

A population is considered a complete set of cases or elements from which a sample is taken and not necessarily be people (Saunders et al., 2015). For this doctoral study, the population was five international development project companies based in the UAE. The sample size was limited to those organizations providing permission to collect data within the proposed population. Therefore, the number of participants was also subject to the population and sampling size. The specific business problem is during an international development project; some project managers lack strategies to meet projects' triple constraints of cost, schedule, and scope. Therefore, the number of participants were from the stated population and sampling. The potential number of participants was 1,209, derived from certified PMP members of the PMI UAE Chapter and the PMI UAE Chapter construction project management LinkedIn group. To be included as a potential participant, the project manager must meet the following criteria: (a) have an active PMP certification or pursuing a PMP certification and (b) at least

5 years of experience working in the UAE as an international development project manager. Qualitative research studies tend to be small and provide richly textured and case-oriented information (Barnett et al., 2018). By managing a sample size of five participants, I handled the complexity of the analysis. Of course, if the sample size exceeded five participants, I terminated further interviews once I achieved data saturation.

The selected population was appropriate for this study because research suggests several negative factors impact the international development industry in the UAE (Al Nahyan et al., 2014; Al Nahyan et al., 2019). Examples are environmental conditions, material logistics, human resource allocation, socio-economic conditions, managing stakeholder communication, and a thorough knowledge of project management practices. Therefore, project managers must share which strategies can overcome those negative impacts to meet or exceed project goals. The implication for positive social change included the opportunity to promote personal development for project managers, improve the employment rate, contribute to a healthier and safer environment for workers, workers' families, and their respective communities.

The most appropriate sampling method was the snowball technique to obtain referrals from persons I know who can also vouch for my character and the importance of this research. According to Ghaljaie et al. (2017), the snowball sampling method involves research participants introducing other people to participate in the study, thus allowing the researcher to conduct a more thorough evaluation. The snowball sampling method was a valuable method to use as I reached out to PMI UAE Chapter members who referred me to their network of professionals that matched the target criteria. I continued to use the snowball sampling method until the data was saturated.

Lastly, I interviewed the participants in a private and secured bedroom in my home office. I conducted virtual one-to-one interviews using the web-based videoconferencing platform Zoom. I asked the participants to be in a quiet setting, preferably their home office, if possible, to focus on the interview without any distractions. Researchers should be cognizant of the quality of virtual conference calls (Cook et al., 2020). The UAE, although still a developing country, has high-quality, high-speed internet and access to video conferencing software.

4

Nature of the Study

Yin (2018) identified three methods for conducting research: mixed methods, qualitative, and quantitative. Mixed-methods researchers combine qualitative and quantitative data collection techniques and analytical procedures (Saunders et al., 2015). To explore project managers' strategies in the international development sector, I relied on the qualitative approach by itself; therefore, I did not use a mixed-methods approach for the study. Qualitative researchers seek to identify meanings of participants' experiences, using various data collection techniques and analytical procedures, to develop a conceptual framework and theoretical contribution (Saunders et al., 2015). I selected the qualitative method to obtain an in-depth understanding of project managers' strategic thinking using rich data and thick descriptions working within international development projects. The data retrieved from a qualitative study enabled me to discover the underlying reasons, motivations, and insights to answer the research question. Researchers use a quantitative research method to examine relationships among variables and group differences, which are analyzed numerically using a range of statistical and graphical techniques (Saunders et al., 2015). Because I did not examine such relationships, I did not select the quantitative research method.

Saunders et al. (2015) described four types of qualitative research designs: case study, ethnographic, narrative, and phenomenological. A multiple qualitative case study research design is an in-depth inquiry into a topic or phenomenon within its real-life setting to understand the dynamics of the subject being studied across several organizations (Saunders et al., 2015). I concluded that a multiple-case study research design was the optimal choice design for this doctoral study. The data retrieved using the design described real-world issues within the real-life settings of multiple organizations, thus making it possible to answer the research question. A single-case study would only provide insight into one project. Focusing on one project would be an incomplete assessment of the business problem. Researchers who conduct multiple-case studies are able to more comprehensively explore research questions and advance theory (Gustafsson, 2017).

In contrast, researchers use an ethnographic research design to study the culture or social world of a group (Saunders et al., 2015). Ethnographic researchers gather observational, interview, and documentary data to produce detailed and comprehensive accounts of different social and cultural phenomena (Saunders et al., 2015). In comparison, narrative researchers obtain and explore participants' personal stories and accounts for interpreting an event or sequence of events through interviews (Saunders et al., 2015). I used data from interviews and other data sources to obtain insight on the business strategies used by participants (vs. a complete story of their personal experience); thus, I decided against using the narrative design. Researchers use the phenomenological design to grasp the significance of the participants' lived experiences (Thompson, 2018). A phenomenological design was not appropriate for this study because the goal was not to study the personal meanings of participants' lived experiences. I used a multiple-case study design to study the business problem in depth.

5

Research Question & Interview Questions

What strategies do project managers use to meet the cost, schedule, and scope of international development projects?

Interview Questions

1. What strategies are you using to identify and address your organization's international development projects' triple constraints?
2. Based upon your organization's experiences, what were the primary causes of your international development projects' failing to meet their quality-related goals?
3. Based upon your organization's experiences, what were the primary causes of our international development projects' exceeding their budgets?
4. Based on your organization's experiences, what were the primary causes of your international development projects' delays?

5. What method(s) did you find worked best to motivate your stakeholders to communicate and address international development projects' triple constraints with each other?
6. How have you found success in meeting the triple constraints of your past international development projects?
7. How are you finding success in meeting the triple constraints of your current international development projects?
8. How, if at all, has the theory of constraints assisted you in your international development projects' success?
9. What else can you share with me about your organization's success strategies and processes in addressing global development projects' triple constraints?

6

Conceptual Framework

The conceptual framework for this study was the theory of constraints (TOC). A project's success is often measured based on the triple constraints, or iron triangle, of time, cost, and scope objectives (Isharyanto et al., 2015). The TOC, developed by Eliyahu M. Goldratt in 1984, is a management philosophy that is focused on identifying and addressing the potential weakest link(s) to improve the structuring and strategy of performance systems. Using the theory can change the ways managers address potential and actual problems related to projects. A tenet of the TOC is that a system constraint limits a system from achieving higher performance versus its goal. To turn the system's constraint into a workable procedure, program and project managers must understand how reality is perceived and addressed (Goldratt, 1999). Therefore, the TOC may provide the insights needed to determine why project and program managers meet or fail to complete the project's goals. Figure 1 is a graphical depiction of the steps in the TOC process. The figure illustrates how program and project managers can use the TOC to identify

15

the critical constraints and opportunities where constraints can be removed or avoided altogether.

Figure 1

Graphical Model of the Theory of Constraints as a Process

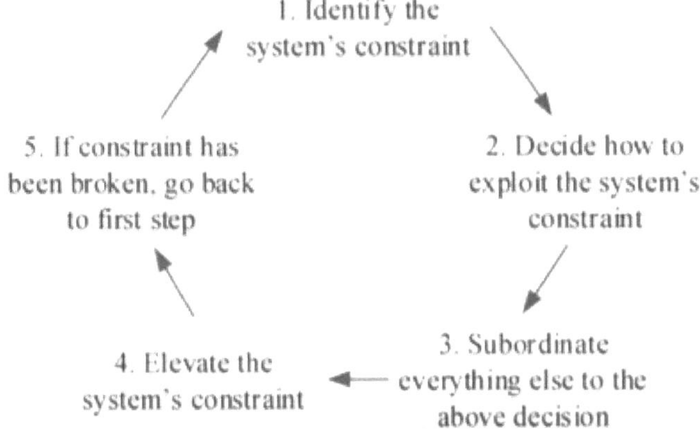

Note. This graphical model illustrates the theory of constraints as a five-step process. From *What Is This Thing Called Theory of Constraints and How Should It Be Implemented?*, by E. M. Goldratt, 1999, North River Press. Copyright 1999 by Dr. Eliyahu Goldratt.

7

Operational Definitions

ecomposition: A technique used for dividing and subdividing the project scope and project deliverables into smaller, more manageable parts (Project Management Institute [PMI], 2017).

Iron triangle: A term used for the three main areas of a project: time, cost, and quality (PMI, 2017).

8

Assumptions, Limitations, and Delimitations

Assumptions

Assumptions are suppositions that the researcher accepts as accurate without concrete proof and that serve as the necessary foundation of any proposed research (Ellis & Levy, 2009). I assumed that participants would understand the interview questions and answer questions accurately and truthfully. Another assumption was that project managers in the study would know and understand strategies to meet projects' cost, schedule, and scope.

Limitations

Limitations are potential weaknesses or problems with the study that are identified by the researcher; they constitute an uncontrollable threat to the internal validity of a study

(Creswell, 2005, p. 198; Ellis & Levy, 2009). The limitation of this study was the participants' potential reluctance to share adverse outcomes of their projects. The participants may have been unwilling to share real results that might have given a negative impression of their capabilities.

Delimitations

Delimitations refer to the bounds or scope of the study. Delimitations are the factors, constructs, and variables that a researcher intentionally leave out of the study, impacting the study's external validity or generalizability (Ellis & Levy, 2009). Participation in this study was delimited to certified project managers working in the UAE on international development projects. Because of the unique nature of the UAE global development industry, I recommend that further research be conducted in another geographical area. Another delimitation was the qualifications of the study participants. To solicit experts' views on project strategies, I only interviewed project managers who possessed PMI's Project Management Professional (PMP) certification or were pursuing PMP certification with at least 5 years of experience. Because many project managers working in the field may not hold a certification, I recommend that future research be conducted with individuals with more hands-on experience.

9

Significance of the Study

Organizations' owners are financially invested in projects, and their main goal is for each project to be completed on time and within budget, while meeting or exceeding the scope requirements. This doctoral study may provide insights and guidance for program and project leaders to meet their projects' triple constraints. Projects are successful when all three areas of the triple constraints equate to more profit for the business. Projects exceeding and failing any of the three areas of the triple constraints cause a monetary loss for the company (Cox & Schleier, 2010). International development projects are complex and require specific skill sets from project managers and other stakeholders.

The first implication for positive social change is the potential for catalyzing better communication with different cultures. The study findings may highlight strategies that project managers can use to improve their understanding of cultural differences. Improved communication may extend beyond the business environment and into the community setting potentially reducing conflict. Another implication for positive social change is the potential mitigation of negative impacts associated with the triple constraints. With fewer negative impacts, organizational leaders may be able to develop long-lasting business relationships, increase global investment opportunities, and increase their projects' overall success rate. Businesses placed in a more advantageous position may boost job creation, positively impacting the communities they serve. Last, project managers may contribute new leadership skills and strategies to future projects.

10

A Review of the Professional and Academic Literature

The following section is a review of professional and academic literature. The work analyzed in the review explain the TOC's relationship and specific business problems. I categorized the literature into three topic groups: (a) challenges with the triple constraints, (b) TOC strategy to address constraint challenges, and (c) benefits as a result of implementing the TOC. The key topics explain the strategies that project managers use to ensure the success of international development projects.

The literature search strategy involved searching Walden University Library databases, PMI's online knowledge bases (available at https://www.pmi.org/and https://www.proje ctmanagement.com/), and Google Scholar. PMI offers its members a knowledge database of published research sources on its main website. In addition, members also can access the ProjectManagement.com website, which includes published resources, webinars, and practitioner listings that can be used for doctoral research. I also reviewed the references included in the peer-reviewed articles I found as well as contributing authors in the project management community and project management journals. Advanced searches were conducted in Walden University library databases employing terms such as

- *project management AND the theory of constraints,*
- *international development projects,*
- *triple constraints of project management,*
- *theory of constraints,* and
- *process improvement strategy for international development projects.*

I filtered the search results to include peer-reviewed sources that were published after 2018 to meet the doctoral study's timeline requirements. If the database I searched did not provide access to the full article, I searched Google Scholar for the full article. The review of the professional and academic literature includes a total of 110 references, most of which (n = 106) are peer-reviewed journal articles. The majority of the peer-reviewed articles (n = 76)) are in the 2018–2022 date range. Thirty-three of the sources are older than 5 years. Three are books that were published between 1998 and 2014. Following the Walden University (2021) DBA rubric and handbook requirements, 70% of the articles were published within the past 5 years. Table 1 provides a summary of the sources that appear in the literature review.

Table 1

Literature Review Sources

Reference type	> 5 years	< 5 years	Total
Peer-reviewed journal articles	30	76	106
Dissertations and non-peer-reviewed journal articles	0	0	0
Books	3	1	4
Government or corporate websites	0	0	0
Total	33	77	110

Purpose of Study

The purpose of this qualitative multiple-case study was to explore the strategies project managers use to successfully meet the triple constraints of cost, schedule, and scope to achieve the goals of international development projects. The targeted population consisted of project managers employed at five international development projects within the UAE who have implemented successful strategies to meet projects' triple constraints.

Theory of Constraints Overview

Goldratt, an Israeli physicist, developed the TOC. The TOC combines systems and constraints principles to leverage change within an organization (Goldratt, 1999). Techt (2014) defined a system as a totality of independent functions that convert the input to output. Techt also described constraint as the weakest link in a chain. Therefore, the TOC uses the constraints in correlation to business systems as starting points for effective changes affecting the organization (Dalei et al., 2019; Techt, 2014; Urban, 2019; Wang & Zhou, 2022). The TOC has five focusing steps (5FS):

1. Identify the constraint.
2. Decide how to optimize the use of the constraint.
3. Subordinate everything else to this decision.
4. Elevate the constraint.
5. Start over if the constraint shifts.

Within the 5FS, managers and employees can quickly identify the constraint(s) after asking the right questions. Once the employee determines the constraint, managers must verify if the constraint is used at its most optimal capacity. For example, the loss of retail store sales due to low inventory stock levels is an example of a negative constraint. Managers need to solve low inventory issues, so customers are not negatively impacted. Step 3 is often the most difficult to complete as it requires all rules, processes, key performance indicators, and so forth to be verified and adapted (Techt, 2014). Once managers complete Steps 2 and 3, the constraint's elevation usually impacts costs or investments. Last, constraints can shift, causing less throughput. Managers must address this situation immediately and start the process over.

The three key performance indicators project managers use to drive decision-making for the TOC are (a) throughput, the difference between sales revenue and necessary total variable costs, (b) inventory/investments, and (c) operating expense (Techt, 2014). Therefore, in Goldratt's theory, one can calculate each business decision based on the influence the decision has on the key performance indicators. However, project managers must not ignore nonconstraints as lacking in importance. Ignoring a nonconstraint impacts the entire business system (Cox & Boyd, 2020; Cox & Schleier, 2010). The more constraints, the better, which does not hold true for the vast majority of system elements, the nonconstraints. Interdependencies exist with the constraints and cannot be determined by solely examining the nonconstraint (Cox & Schleier, 2010). An increase in nonconstraints does not necessarily equate to better business system performance. Business leaders must focus on what should be done, not on what should not be done (Cox & Schleier, 2010).

Theory of Constraints Thinking Processes

Goldratt also used scientific thinking methods outside of the traditional sciences such as general management, manufacturing management, management information systems, etc. (McMullen, 1998; Urban, 2019). Thus, Goldratt invented the structured TOC thinking processes, which take the form of the TOC logic tree management processes allowing the method to be effective for day-to-day use (McMullen, 1998). According to Dalei et al. (2019), the thinking processes contain a set of five logic diagrams. The logic trees are the current reality tree, future reality tree, transition tree, prerequisite tree, and the evaporating cloud (Banerjee & Lowalekar, 2021; Dalei et al., 2019; Vijaykar, 2021).

The need for a logical, detailed structure to follow the TOC led to the development of the refinement of the thinking processes of the TOC from 1989 to 1992 (Cox & Boyd, 2020; Cox & Schleier, 2010). Thinking processes of the TOC contributes to finding the root cause of the problem (Lacerda et al., 2014; Urban, 2019). Combining TOC modeling processes and thinking processes leads to a systematic view of the issues encountered and process improvement redesign (Cristovão et al., 2019; Lacerda et al., 2014; Punb & Ragbir, 2018; Urban, 2019). Techt (2014) argued that five targets lead the TOC business strategy's thinking processes; the potential to earn money, excited markets, ongoing improvement, secure employment, and profitable growth are mandatory strategic objectives. In summary, the TOC, combined with thinking processes, equates to anything's physics (McMullen, 1998). Project managers view the TOC thinking processes as a problem-solving method that offers win-win solutions to overcoming obstacles (Cox, 2021; Cox & Schleier, 2010; see also Lacerda et al., 2014).

Although Goldratt developed the TOC based on a manufacturing business model, other business leaders have tried to implement the same practices due to its success in the manufacturing environment. This has required some modification. In these other applications, constraints in project environments are not referred to as *bottlenecks*; they are called *critical paths/chains*. In distribution-based organizations, the bottlenecks are wholesalers and retailers. Hence a *bottleneck* is used interchangeably with a *constraint*.

The constraint moves with the market in operations, and organizations' sales and competitive edge increase with improvements. Competitive advantage is increased based on the company satisfying the demand need more than its competitors (Cox & Schleier, 2010). Leaders focused on capitalizing on the competitive edge rather than refining operations, thus focusing on strategy. However, the development of this type of laser focus on strategy can cause constraints as sales increase. The thinking process of the TOC has to be holistically implemented by project managers to synchronize sales and operations properly. Business leaders who focus on the process of ongoing improvement can capitalize and sustain their companies. Growth should not degrade the stability of the organization. Hence, the most powerful tool is the strategy and tactic tree. Strategy is the answer to "what for?," and tactic is the answer to "how?" (Cox & Schleier, 2010).

Cox and Schleier (2010) argued that S&T trees achieve three objectives: (a) bring clarity to implementations, (b) enhance communication through the management levels, and (c) achieve synchronization between the various departments. Stratton and Yeong (2017) argued S&T trees are a change management tool used by operations and management practitioners in TOC to capture and increase the TOC generalization. Project managers use S&T trees to create and implement a change with a series of inquiries (i.e., why the change is needed, what strategy will be used for a specific, measurable objective, why a particular tactic makes the goal possible, how to best achieve the tactic, and what advice should be given to subordinates may jeopardize the tactic's sufficiency; Stratton & Yeong, 2017).

Knowledge is generated throughout the change process, while embedded assumptions are necessary, parallel, and sufficient (Mihić et al., 2020; Stratton & Yeong, 2017).

Harmony (2016) argued the application of strategic planning and execution processes does not address the root cause(s) of high failure rates. Organizational change initiatives average a success rate of 20–40%, with high failure rates not improving over time (Harmony, 2016). However, the S&T should be a simple, logical tree of hierarchy of the high leverage changes and their respective implementation sequences (Harmony, 2016). Harmony (2016) discussed two levels of strategy and tactics. Level 1 strategy represents the organization's growth target, and Level 1 tactic represents a summary of the main changes top management should focus on defining their priority (Harmony, 2016). Level 2 strategy and tactics represent the organization's highest leverage changes to achieve its growth target successfully and sustainably (Harmony, 2016). The caveat is the strategy and tactic are only as valid as the assumptions they are based on; therefore, at every level, a manager must define and communicate the strategy and tactic for each proposed change and its logic (Harmony, 2016).

Project Management Methodology

Accordingly, project managers view project success on another set of similar metrics named constraints. Project constraints are costs, quality, risk, schedule, scope, and resources. Schedule, cost, and scope, also known as the iron triangle with quality at the center of the triangle, are considered the most critical factors determining project success according to PMI's (2017)

A Guide to the Project Management Body of Knowledge: PMBOK guide (*PMBOK*). The importance of each constraint varies for each project, causing project managers to tailor their approach for managing each constraint. Project managers consider different governance levels, organizational culture, and if the customer is internal or external when making managerial decisions (Dan-asabe et al., 2020; Ebrahimzadeh et al., 2019; PMI, 2017). The *PMBOK* is not a methodology but is considered a resource for recommendations and good practice for tailoring to achieve a project's specific needs (PMI, 2017).

As projects operate within the organization's constraints, project managers develop a project management plan, a comprehensive document defining the basis of all project work, referencing the iron triangle's baseline elements and how the work will be performed (PMI, 2017). Subsidiary plans are the cost management plan, schedule management plan, and scope management plan. Sapiuly (2017) suggested the strategic management plan minimizes the negative consequences of economic crisis for oil and gas companies in Kazakhstan and other countries with more research. The cost, schedule, and scope baselines are the approved versions of the models used as a basis for comparison to actual results (PMI, 2017). Failure results from at least one of the three constraints not meeting their expectations.

In some cases, two or even all three constraints do not meet expectations. The project manager's goal is to balance the competing constraints with the available resources (PMI, 2017). In contrast, March et al. (2018) argued transforming project management knowledge into process theories will advance the science of project management while strengthening the link between theory and practice. Viewing project management as a process theory will help project managers comprehend the various issues with constraints and communicate the how and why of the results (March et al., 2018; Mihić et al., 2020).

In comparison, Li et al. (2020) argued international project managers must first have a set of competencies to function in the global development work environment. Project management goal-oriented competencies guide project managers to undertake the decision-making among cost, resource, quality, and time constraints both in traditional and international projects (Kozhakhmetova et al., 2019; Li et al., 2020). However, project management methods, processes, techniques, and tools can promote project success in the global development industry (Ika et al., 2020; Li et al., 2020). International projects in emerging and developing countries require different competencies due to their high uncertainty and complexity (Carral et al., 2018; Ika et al., 2020; Li et al., 2020; Paulmakesh & Yimer, 2021). Project managers should conduct uncertainty management through proactive planning, adaptation, and routinization (Li et al., 2020). Solving complex problems and understanding international standards require expert knowledge (Li et al., 2020).

Triple Constraint Challenges

Briére and Proulx (2013) explained in international development, project success is vital because of beneficiary countries' socioeconomic goals. International development projects' objectives are less tangible and measurable than the conventional or commercial project types due to their not-for-profit nature (Auclair & Brière, 2020; Corti et al., 2017). Authors

Alashwal et al. (2017) stated international construction projects are swarmed with various challenges, leading to enormous economic consequences. For example, 50% of construction projects in the UAE are delayed and not completed on schedule (Mainga, 2017). Schedule overruns affected close to 95% of Abu Dhabi and Dubai (Mainga, 2017). In Malaysia, design changes during an international development project contribute to project delay, and cost increases up to 20% (Yap et al., 2017; Dohl et al., 2021). Haque et al. (2021) noted that 100% of green building projects have increased project costs, with lack of communication another challenge in 84% of projects.

Despite the gloomy statistics, the advantages of venturing into the international market include increased profits, efficient resource utilization, growth and development, and a competitive advantage over local contractors (Alashwal et al., 2017; Armenia et al., 2019). Such challenges are a lack of shared vision and commitment to the project by the team and the stakeholders, competitiveness, poorly defined, unrealistic, and out of date planning impacting the project schedule, inadequate analysis of the risk factors, bureaucratic management by the donor, lack of resources, lack of internal feedback, and an approach omitting local knowledge from the rollout of a project (Alashwal et al., 2017; Briére & Proulx, 2013; Charkhakan & Heravi, 2019; de Carvalho & Santos, 2021; Ebrahimzadeh et al., 2019). Researchers found those elements impacting the success of a project are categorized into four main groups which are 1) the involvement of the stakeholders throughout the project lifecycle, 2) achieving results, 3) project impact, and 4) project team skillset, implementation, and management of projects in the community (Briére & Proulx, 2013; Dan-asabe et al., 2020; de Carvalho & Santos, 2021; Kamu & Paul, 2018). Stakeholders are the decision-makers, financially responsible, and have defined the project's scope and requirements. Not being involved throughout the project's lifecycle leads to negative impacts, which affects the scope. Therefore, project team members must have the necessary skill set to achieve the results required. For example, according to Al Nahyan et al. (2019), a crucial skill for managers of construction projects is to manage stakeholders' expectations. The projects fail because construction stakeholders have the necessary resources and decision power to stop the project. Discordance among stakeholders delegating decision-making authority is common in international development projects (Al Nahyan et al., 2021; Picciotto, 2020). They can influence cost, time, performance, and stakeholder satisfaction. Based on the authors' research, schedule delays, financial loss, and project failure result from cultural issues such as trust and fear, lack of participation and commitment, poor communication and planning, transparent tasks and expectations, and knowledge/information sharing (Ahmed, 2019; Kozhakhmetova et al., 2019; Mihić et al., 2020; Ngala et al., 2020). However, Messner (2015) argued organizations should invest in global team dynamics to understand their international teams' strengths and deficiencies. By investing in this cultural coaching, managers will find the root cause of team conflicts and performance problems (Messner, 2015).

Similarly, in a scenario where political corruption is the main factor in project failure, Damoah et al. (2018) revealed that the Ghanaian government's corrupt practices cause total abandonment, cost deviation, time overrun, and requirements deviation government projects. Project managers and their respective contractors are at the mercy of government-appointed project leaders who demand bribes. If the contractors refuse to pay those bribes, those leaders create havoc for the project, leading to abandonment (Damoah et al., 2018). Participants also stated corruption leads to a negative impact on costs, specifically cost escalation. Examples of cost escalation include government officials and contractors increasing prices to share the profits or intermediaries who have relationships with government officials who can guarantee government contracts for a fee. Banker et al. (2018) described this type of behavior as a psychological bias which opens up a "black box" of cost behavior. Damoah et al. argued corrupt practices also lead to negative impacts on the project schedule. Contractors deliberately delay projects, also causing costs to escalate. Government officials, subject matter experts, and consultants demand money and other resources before certifying the projects' progress, thus influencing delays (Damoah et al., 2018). Damoah et al.'s research also revealed Ghanaian government project deliverables do not meet scope requirements due to lack of supervision by consultants and quality control officers and the use of cheaper, substandard materials. Lastly, Damoah et al. argued once corruption affects the project's management phase, it produces a ripple effect on the stakeholders. Government project leaders are hired to represent the people in a developing country (Damoah et al., 2018). Citizens cannot reap the benefits of development projects, leading to economic and social hardships. Unfortunately, the there is no straightforward technique used by project managers to prevent corruption (Ameyaw et al., 2019). Chang et al. (2018) recommended six strategy-based components to manage political risk management scenarios described by Damoah et al. Developing innovative techniques are essential to the triple constraints of cost, schedule, and scope for international development projects (Ameyaw et al., 2019).

Meanwhile, Pollack et al. (2018) stated that the iron triangle concept (cost, schedule, and quality) effectively communicates the criteria' interrelationship. Movement in one constraint naturally puts pressure on the other constraint. Reliance on the iron triangle increases when projects become complex in scope leading to cost and schedule overruns (Pollack et al., 2018; Wang & Zhou, 2022). Time and cost are interrelated because the expenses increase with the increase in time or delay in progress (Banker et al., 2018; Vignesh & Vijayabanu, 2018; Wang & Zhou, 2022). Customer value is another relationship closely connected to scope management with the customer's perception of satisfaction with the results and the perception of the customer's cost (Al-Rubaiei et al., 2018; Álvarez-Pérez et al., 2018). During the early phases of a project, schedule, cost, and quality are in order of importance. As the project progresses forward, cost and schedule are significant challenges.

Mainga (2017) argued that project managers create constraint challenges from time pressures towards the end of the project, an increased focus on short-term project deliverables, and fear of adverse reactions when disclosing mistakes leading to projects' knowledge transfer inhibited. Once the project is complete, quality supersedes the other constraints. Researchers mentioned in Pollack et al.'s (2018) article critiqued the validity of the triple constraints stating the iron triangle simplifies project work perception, leading to the anxiety of overcoming project outcomes. However, the triple constraints are of great importance cannot illustrate complete project success (Pollack et al., 2018). Pollack et al.'s research showed project planning has become less significant concerning all three constraints, while the control has become less significant with cost and quality. The researchers also state that project managers' progress towards the project objectives, decision-making, and decision support must be emphasized (Pollack et al., 2018). Especially in the construction industry, project success goes beyond the objectives within the triple constraints and includes safety, resource efficiency, effectiveness, stakeholder satisfaction, and conflict resolution (Pollack et al., 2018). Pollack et al. argued the relevance of time, cost, and quality is contingent on the project context. However, if viewing the iron triangle as an educational tool, Pollack et al. argued variations in project duration or budget could affect variations in scope, meeting requirements, and the standard of created deliverables. Scope, performance, requirements, and quality could be interchangeable as the third vertex in the iron triangle based on the project type (Pollack et al., 2018).

In contrast, authors Pretorius et al. (2012) stated the project management iron triangle is one of the most overlooked project management fundamentals. However, it demonstrates the consequences of change on the triple constraint. Project Managers cannot change the iron triangle's three elements without impacting each other (Pretorius et al., 2012; Wang & Zhou, 2022). In 2012, the project management literature lacked scholarship on the triple constraint and its dynamics, resulting in project managers not effectively prioritizing and exploiting the triple constraint trade-offs (Pretorius et al., 2012). Project managers fail to address the strategy ambiguity or establish tangible project goals (Charkhakan & Heravi, 2019; Pretorius et al., 2012). Another challenge project managers face is infringing on customer requirements. Pretorius et al. define a project by listing the triple constraint variables to flexibility. For the project to succeed, the exploitation of flexibility in the weaker constraints project managers use meets the least flexible constraint (Pretorius et al., 2012). The middle constraint has minimal flexibility and can move towards the weakest or strongest constraint, enacting a power struggle. However, failure to deliver all three constraints variables on target does not necessarily equate to project failure (Pretorius et al., 2012).

Additionally, Acar et al. (2018) argued constraints could influence creativity and innovation. The constraints are categorized differently as input, output, and process constraints. Acar et al. defined input constraints as the unavailability of resources such as time, human resources, funds, excess cash, and materials used in the service of creativity and innovation. Process constraints determine the steps to be followed throughout the creativity and innovation processes (Acar et al., 2018; Chong & Heath, 2021). Acar et al.'s research suggested that process constraints negatively affect organizational behavior and are detrimental to creativity and innovation's motivational mechanisms. However, process constraints may contribute to innovation in the technology and operations management industries by facilitating communication and coordination on deliverables (Acar et al., 2018; Ahmed, 2019; Chong & Hearth, 2021). Output constraints are the factors project managers use to define the creative processes, such as the scope requirements.

Meanwhile, Acar et al. (2018) developed a slightly different understanding of constraints based on their specific type and enforcement, malleability, and project creativity and innovation timing. A constraint has an enforcement characteristic referring to the incentives used to ensure compliance. An example of the enforced constraint is through regulations banning the use of specific materials such as the International

Airport and Transportation Association's banning of standalone lithium batteries on passenger aircraft, altering logistic operations for technology giants such as Apple, Microsoft, etc. A constraint has a malleability characteristic referring to the extent of its flexibility. Lastly, a constraint's timing refers to how a constraint could be imposed or altered at the beginning of an innovation process, which may affect the outcome of said process. Acar et al. (2018) stated the key to creativity and innovation is not to remove all constraints nor focus on a single type of constraint.

Strategies Based on the Theory of Constraints

Business owners first applied the TOC in production planning and scheduling, identifying which key constraint positively or negatively impacted the project (Goldratt, 1999; Jugend et al., 2018; Jugend et al., 2019). Golmohammadi (2015) conducted a quantitative case study involving an automotive parts manufacturing operation based on a job-shop production system. Golmohammadi chose this particular case study because the job shop system had complex operational workflows, which created many shifting constraints. Second, the system's complexity provided an excellent environment for testing the value of using a master production schedule (MPS) based on the TOC scheduling systems and the impact of varying resource utilization levels on operations performance. Next, the case study researcher analyzed the effect of several factors throughout, and fourth, the role of free products in scheduling can be investigated. Based on the results of the production-based study, implementing the TOC was not the proper solution. Eliminating or reducing the effect of one constraint ultimately led to the increase of another constraint. Golmohammadi acknowledged the research limitation due to one complex production case's sample size. Additional cases of the same characteristics need further validation. Similarly, the use of TOC is not novel for healthcare systems, argues Bauer et al. (2019). However, Bauer et al. researched examples of companies implementing the TOC thinking processes that eliminated or reduced scheduling issues, reduced waste, reduced hospital costs, and increased patient satisfaction.

In contrast, the TOC's logic is based upon the effect-cause-effect relationship and the critical vision of reality, which seeks to identify why things happen and not how they happen (Bauer et al., 2019; Lacerda et al., 2014). A Strategy and Tactic Tree (S&T) change management tool, often used by operations and management-based organizations, captures, and proliferates the TOC body of knowledge (Stratton & Yeong, 2017). S&T trees is an inquiry process into making a change with a series of questions embracing the mapping of cause-and-effect logic using abductive reasoning, which are fundamental qualities of what information holds precedence (Stratton & Yeong, 2017).

Project managers utilize the foundations of TOC in various process tools related to project management. According to the mixed method case study by authors Dostatni and Trojanowska (2017), a project management method called Critical Chain Project Management (CCPM) was developed in 1997 by Goldratt on the foundations of the TOC. Goldratt created the CCPM to address the problems associated with Gantt charts and CPM (Critical Path Method) formed in 1957 (Jugend et al., 2018; Jugend et al., 2019). The critical chain refers to the most extended sequence of dependent tasks derived from the resources (Techt, 2014). CCPM consists of planning, scheduling, and maintaining the critical chain during the project to maximize the bottleneck's working time and efficiently determine inventories for the fundamentals (Dostatni & Trojanowska, 2017). A time buffer is often added at the end of a CCPM project because project managers consider both precedence and resource dependencies (Soltani & Zohrehvandi, 2022).

Similarly, authors Izmailov et al. (2016) stated that CCPM is a tool used in one-project and multi-project structures where resources are used simultaneously in several projects. For multi-project structures, this tool includes all the elements of the same tool designed in a one-project structure, plus a tool to synchronize the implementation of projects, which can be either physical (resource) or virtual (no more than six projects) (Izmailov et al., 2016; Melendez et al., 2018). Anholon et al. (2019) argued multitasking does not affect the system's performance as the critical resource's effect was protected by eliminating conflicts between resources and balancing the distribution of shared resources per the CCPM method. However, Cox and Schleier (2010) argued that buffers control new projects' initiation once project managers establish project priorities. Soltani & Zohrehvandi (2022) argued when project managers incorporate buffers, it leads to changes in project scheduling causing delivery delay. Multi-project environments have no regard for resource usage in other projects, and therefore, the entry of new projects into the system must be maintained (Cox & Schleier, 2010). Cox and Schleier recommended a scheduling resource to minimize resource conflicts and prevent constricting the organization with too many projects executed simultaneously. Holweg and Maylor

(2018) also stated megaprojects transform organizations with their budgetary size, extent, and organizational complexity. Hasan et al. (2016) argued the paradox of megaproject performance needs to be addressed beyond the triple constraints but rather extend the dimensions of project success towards customer impact, team impact, business success, and future planning. Future planning includes new technology, market, product lines, core competency, and organizational capability to increase competitiveness (Cantarelli & Genovese, 2021; Hasan et al., 2016; Laishram & Thounaojam, 2021).

The Gantt chart, developed as a production control tool in 1917 by Henry L. Gantt, provides a graphical illustration of a schedule project managers use to plan, coordinate, and track project deliverables (Dostatni & Trojanowska, 2017). Furthermore, project managers use the CPM method to estimate the minimum project duration and determine the schedule flexibility on the schedule model's logical network paths (PMI, 2017). The CPM is also used to calculate the critical paths(s) and schedule flexibility on the schedule model's logical network paths (PMI, 2017). Project managers use traditional project management practices to protect the project schedule by building buffers for each deliverable, however some researchers suggest creating a more realistic and reliable schedule (Chileshe & Kavishe, 2018; Park, 2021; Soltani & Zohrehvandi, 2022; Techt, 2014).

In contrast, safety buffers are removed from each deliverable in the critical path method and placed at the end of the critical chain (Techt, 2014). When project managers move buffers to the end of the critical chain, they create a safety net for all contingencies, which places the project schedule at risk (Techt, 2014). The downside of moving buffers to the end of the project is the loss of change requests (Techt, 2014).

In summary, the constraint of achieving the organization's goal is the real strength of the TOC. The TOC provides the 5FS (five focusing steps) to identify the constraint and the S&T (strategy and tactic) trees to communicate the detailed steps and expected results while thinking processes provide solutions if you are unable to solve one of the 5FS (Cox & Boyd, 2020; Cox & Schleier, 2010). Creasy et al. (2016) argued business owners should not refer to the TOC as a theory but as an innovation and a "management of constraints" to reduce project duration before creating a critical chain path.

Strategies Based on Project Management Principles

Any project needs an effective team, management with high competence, and project management mastery to succeed (Annany et al., 2018). According to Jokkaw and Tongthong (2017), time, quality, cost, and safety management were the most critical knowledge areas for construction project managers in the Thailand region. Donnelly and Ika (2017) argued project management standards and guidelines alone would not automatically lead to project success nor the positive impact on the triple constraints, stakeholders, and the project beneficiaries. However, project management utilized as a strategy is a set of management skills, knowledge, and tools required for project activities to meet the project constraints' requirements (Annany et al., 2018; Kamu & Paul, 2018). Cox and Schleier confirmed using a systems perspective of focusing on core problems of project failures might cause more problems. Project management strategies are similar to the

TOC in this regard. Recognize all the activities required to achieve a project's goal and the organization, ensuring the project scope aligns with the system (Callistus & Clinton, 2018; Cox & Schleier, 2010).

The PMI's *PMBOK* provides a foundation for project managers to tailor their projects' needs called knowledge areas. The iron triangle knowledge areas are project scope management, project schedule management, project cost management, and project quality management. Project scope management ensures the project includes all the necessary work and the necessary work to complete (Al-Rubaueu et al., 2018; PMI, 2017). The step-by-step scope management process comprises planning, collecting requirements, defining the scope, creating deliverables, validating scope, and controlling scope (PMI, 2017). Best practices for scope management include

- determine problems and identify business needs;
- identify and recommend viable solutions for meeting those needs;
- elicit, document, and manage stakeholder requirements; and
- facilitate the successful implementation of the program or project's product, service, or end result (PMI, 2017).

For example, integrated construction companies agree on scope and quality specifications when executing projects. In contrast, non-integrated construction companies tend to use the scope and quality buffers as a tool to optimize the cost and time of the project (Molenaar et al., 2019). Contrary to the scope management guidelines, Molenaar et al. (2019) argue non-integrated construction project managers do not typically share with the client the excessive scope or quality buffers detected in the specifications. However, according to Vereijssen et al. (2017), two coinnovation principles primarily affect the project's focus and direction; the first principle is to take the time to understand the problem from different angles, and the second is to be inclusive in terms of diversity of stakeholders. Thus, Vereijssen et al. argued with Molenaar et al. on which stakeholders receive information.

Project schedule management includes the processes required to manage the project's timely completion (PMI, 2017). The step-by-step process for schedule management includes planning schedule management, defining activities, sequence activities, estimating activity durations, developing the schedule, and controlling the schedule (PMI, 2017). Best practices for schedule management include

- iterative schedule with a backlog,
- on-demand scheduling,
- life-cycle approach,
- resource availability,
- project dimensions, and
- technology support (PMI, 2017).

Project cost management involves planning, estimating, budgeting, financing, funding, managing, and controlling costs within the approved budget (PMI, 2017). A project's success or failure depends on the project manager's ability to properly estimate cost (Elshwadfy & Ibrahim, 2021). The step-by-step process for cost management includes planning cost management, estimating costs, determining a budget, and controlling costs (PMI, 2017). Best practices for tailoring the project cost management process include

- knowledge management,
- estimating and budgeting,
- earned value management,
- use of an agile approach, and
- governance (PMI, 2017).

Project quality management is the process of incorporating the organization's quality policy regarding planning, managing, and controlling project and product quality requirements to meet stakeholders' expectations (PMI, 2017). The step-by-step process for quality management includes planning, managing, and controlling quality. Best practices for project quality management include

- customer satisfaction,
- continual improvement,
- management responsibility,
- mutually beneficial partnership with suppliers,
- policy compliance and auditing,
- standard and regulatory compliance, and
- stakeholder engagement (PMI, 2017).

Total quality management encourages cost reduction, creating high-quality goods and services, customer satisfaction, employee empowerment, and measuring results (Ganguly, 2019). "The most common active acceptance strategy is to establish a contingency reserve, including amounts of time, money, or resources to handle the threat if it occurs" (PMI, 2017, p.443). Project managers commonly use a contingency of money reserves and buffers (Molenaar et al., 2019). However, project managers do not use formal methods but instead establish as much time and cost contingency as project objectives allow them to do, according to Molenaar et al., because they are not the only decision-makers determining contingencies. Once the project managers set the goals, the project manager can adjust accordingly without senior leadership influence.

According to Fernandes et al. (2019), project management is highly contingent on the business structure and the organization's environment. According to project managers in the field, project management bodies of knowledge and standards have three fundamental limitations. They lack empirical foundation, are inventories of practices with little indication of the relative importance of diverse approaches, and indicate project managers must adapt the practice to the context without providing hints of what this adaptation might be (Fernandes et al., 2019). Therefore, project managers cluster practices into four main toolsets: planning/initiating, planning/executing, planning/controlling, and planning/closing. The planning/initiating toolset focuses on the project scope statement and milestone planning (Callistus & Clinton, 2018; Fernandes et al., 2019). The planning/executing toolset identifies risk, the work breakdown structure, planning tools, issue log, lesson learned documents, and implementing tools. The planning/controlling toolset includes several techniques from the monitoring and controlling process groups such as progress reports and meetings, baseline planning, Gantt charts for schedule and scope control, and change requests (Fernandes et al., 2019). The planning/closing toolset consists of four techniques: client acceptance form, close contracts, project closure documents, and an activity list (Fernandes et al., 2019). Project managers strongly link planning practices to the combination of the remaining process groups. Based on Fernandes et al.'s research results, project management is a relatively consistent practice but is dependent on the business sector.

In contrast, Hasan et al. (2016) argued responsible project management (RPM) goes beyond time, cost, and quality constraints. Instead, it is a process carried out by reliable and accountable firms, government agencies, society representatives, and multiple stakeholders. RPM is a cross-disciplinary management process in which stakeholders are responsible for a project and its consequences sustainably (Hasan et al., 2016). As a tool, the RPM process improves organizations' performance while addressing project and mega project's sustainability, amplifying the traditional project management approach's scope and scale. The primary constraint on RPM is the reflection of the implications and consequences of past projects' use of resources (Hasan et al., 2016). By taking a proactive approach to how organizations influence each other and recognizing their complexities and uncertainties, project managers imply a learning system (Hasan et al., 2016). Responsible leaders and stakeholders will transform the decision-making process to improve performance.

Furthermore, global project managers must be human-oriented and relationship-oriented, building trustworthy relationships with local government, industry, and authorities in the country due to their dynamic, complex business processes (Aarseth et al., 2014; Ciric et al., 2019; Ika et al., 2020; Pirju, 2018). Batista et al. (2019) argued beyond strategy, operations, and projects, the stakeholders (clients and employees) should be included as one of the bases for competitive advantage.

Project managers recognize changes with increased flexibility to address those changes; however, stakeholders share the commitment, collaboration, alignment, and adaptation necessary for project success (Ciric et al., 2019; Donnelly & Ika, 2017; Gunduz & Almuajebh, 2020; Ika & Munro, 2020; Ika et al., 2020). Aarseth et al. (2014) identified three project management-based methods for handling organizational challenges. First, develop a global project relationship management plan for recurring problematic stakeholders (see also Gunduz & Almuajebh, 2020). Second, create a global human resources management plan with lessons learned from past projects in different countries (see also Berner et al., 2018; Picciotto, 2020). Resource management also includes the procurement of resources. According to Bhandarkar et al. (2020), there is a need for faster planning as multiple changes in procurement requests can be required at any time during the execution of a project. Lastly, define global systems to align central and international projects in different national settings, including systems and technology necessary for process improvement and consistent communication (Aarseth et al., 2014; see also Ahmed, 2019; Ahsan & Kumar, 2018; Punb & Ragbir, 2018).

Benefits of Theory of Constraints Implementation

According to Isharyanto et al. (2015), there is clear evidence the poor success rate of projects is due in part to poorly managed resources and recognition of constraints. The authors discuss three theories in their conceptual paper, the TOC. The TOC can evaluate obstacles, limitations, and similar problems in a project and develop a breakthrough solution (Isharyanto et al.,

2015). Just as Goldratt described, the objective is to identify the weakest link in the project management plan, exploit the constraint, subordinate all else to the strategy to manage the constraint, elevate the constraint, and if one of the steps fail, start over from Step 1 (Isharyanto et al., 2015; Urban, 2019). By incorporating TOC into the early stages of the project management life cycle, the benefits are reduced delays and project completion within budget, scope, and meeting quality specifications (Isharyanto et al., 2015).

Contrary to Golmohammadi, the authors believe effective project managers provide the foundation for successful project outcomes as they are ultimately responsible for achieving the project objectives (Isharyanto et al., 2015). Isharyanto et al. conducted two case studies (The Channel Tunnel and London Heathrow Terminal 5 airport) to compare TOC elements and two other theories in the project management life cycle to retrieve data to confirm success factors. Both projects were completed successfully and considered international mega-projects incorporating TOC, RBV/RAV, and RDT. In summary, project managers applied the TOC methodology to manage access and site constraints reducing structural, supplier, and socio-political complexities and improving collaboration among project partners (Ballesteros-Sánchez et al., 2020; Isharyanto et al., 2015). The project's implementation following the limits of the pipeline, project planning method, critical chain buffers, and management decisions based on those buffers is a significant acceleration of the project's flow and completion (Izmailov et al., 2016).

Similarly, Grida and Zeid (2019) utilized a system dynamics-based model to implement the TOC within Egypt's healthcare system. Egypt's healthcare system had limited healthcare resources, long service times, and an inability to track patient arrivals. The system dynamics model depends on system thinking, looking at behavior patterns in events, thus evaluating the system's cause-and-effect relationship (Grida & Zeid, 2019). The first step of the TOC is to identify the constraint, which Grida and Zeid identified as the utilization of resources doctors. Doctors are appointed based on the availability of the operating rooms (Grida & Zeid, 2019). Exploiting the constraints involved developing time-based policies. To subordinate the constraint, doctors proposed a bed-sharing approach. To elevate the system's performance, doctors simulate their availability through different percentages (Grida & Zeid, 2019). Grida and Zeid's research showed an overall 6% improvement in the system output a 30% decrease in waiting lists without resource elevation. However, with a 40% elevation in doctor availability, system throughput increases by 13%, with an 88% decrease in the waiting list (Grida & Zeid, 2019).

In contrast, Golmohammadi and Mansouri (2015) argued the process of identifying the bottleneck is not sufficient and accurate for complex operations in real-world systems. Instead, Golmohammadi and Mansouri developed another TOC-based approach utilizing an algorithm called COLOMAPS to generate a master production schedule. COLOMAPS identifies constraints define the complexity of operations and capacity utilization. The critical differentiator between COLOMAPS and the TOC is in COLOMAPS, whose demands exceed their capacities in a static situation as bottlenecks (Golmohammadi & Mansouri, 2015). All resources may play the role of constraints (Golmohammadi & Mansouri, 2015). The authors' results identified the COLOMAPS algorithm leads to better throughput when creating the master production schedule. Golmohammadi and Mansouri also note identifying constraints is not effective within complex, dynamic operations due to a lack of accuracy (Golmohammadi & Mansouri, 2015).

Yet, TOC thinking process tools were considered powerful instruments for uncovering assumptions in the research provided by Mabin and Mirzaei (2017). Project managers utilized TOC thinking processes to facilitate detection and mapping, finding the logic behind differentiating project management methods. Cause-and-effect logic tools helped the researchers understand the project manager during a case study analysis by highlighting wrong assumptions and identifying missing information (Mabin & Mirzaei, 2017). The same logical structure of TOC thinking processes can be used by project managers interchangeably in case study research and project constraint analysis.

Likewise, Dostatni and Trojanowska's (2017) research concluded the implementation of CCPM guided the company to streamline project management processes and improve communication between the company and its stakeholders. Further improvements included timeliness of order delivery, quality of service, and increased customer satisfaction. The company's greatest challenge was the resistance to change by the employees. Equally important, Anholon et al. (2019) tested the capabilities of CCPM implementation in a multi-project system in search of key factors influencing performance. Anholon et al. argued that the CCPM method allows for better workload distribution and facilitates monitoring activities and resource allocation based on their test results. Anholon et al. also concluded multitasking does not affect the system's performance because the bottleneck (critical resources) was protected by eliminating conflicts between resources and balancing shared resources.

Summary

In summary, the TOC combines organizational systems and conditions to leverage change. Practitioners of the theory use the five focusing steps to make sound business decisions related to the triple constraints of cost, schedule, and scope. As manufacturing business leaders continued to adapt the TOC into their daily operations, other industry leaders and project managers realized the need for a more logical structure and strategy to transfer across multiple types of businesses. Goldratt developed the strategy and tactic trees, five thinking process tools used in combination with the TOC system. However, project managers are experts on the project management methodology, which follows a more robust system of constraints.

Similarly, the triple constraints of cost, schedule, and scope significantly influence Project managers' view of the method of project management as a process theory itself, comparably to the TOC. Organizational leaders and project managers implement the TOC thinking processes and project management methodology into their project strategies within the complex international development industry. Corporate leaders and project managers implement a combination of TOC and S&T trees, but project managers also implement CCPM, Gantt charts, PERT, or CPM in conjunction with S&T trees. In addition to TOC strategic methods, project managers execute project management-based strategies such as scope management, schedule management, cost management, and quality management.

Transition

In Section 1 of the doctoral study, I discussed the business problem and described the purpose and nature of the study. The research question and interview questions that I used to address the specific business problem also appear in the section. I also discussed the doctoral study's conceptual framework and its relation to the study's foundation. I noted the study's assumptions, limitations, and delimitations. Last, I reviewed the professional and academic literature and explained the history of TOC and its respective tools while comparing the TOC with project management methodologies. In Section 2, I will discuss my role as the researcher and provide an overview of the methodology. Information on the participants, research method and design, population and sampling, ethical research, data collection instruments and technique, data organization technique, data analysis, and reliability and validity is provided. In Section 3, I will present the research findings and discuss their potential applications to professional practice and implications for positive social change. I also present recommendations for action and further research, reflect on my growth as a researcher and practitioner, and provide a conclusion to the study.

II

The Project

In Section 2, I will provide an overview of the study. I will restate the purpose, explain my role as the researcher, and discuss the research design and method. The population and sampling, ethical procedures, data collection instruments and technique, data organization technique, data analysis, and reliability and validity will also be described.

11

Purpose Statement

The purpose of this qualitative multiple case study was to explore the strategies project managers use to meet international development projects' triple constraints of cost, schedule, and scope. The targeted population comprised project managers employed at five international development projects within the UAE who have implemented successful strategies to meet projects' triple constraints. The implications for positive social change include the opportunity to increase business profitability, which might lead to increased wages for project managers; increased employment; and a healthier and safer environment for workers, workers' families, and their respective communities.

12

Role of the Researcher

As the researcher for the doctoral study and primary data collection instrument, I collected data from participant interviews and PMI's knowledge database. I followed an interview protocol (see Appendix) to ensure data reliability. I assumed consistent professional behavior and demeanor when interviewing each participant. A conversational interview style may lead to a social relationship that results in an individualized interaction with every participant (Yin, 2015). To ensure consistency, I followed an interview protocol when interviewing participants.

As the researcher, I was responsible for negotiating access to the organizations and the participants. As a current project manager with international development experience, I know about the study topic. I have 3 years of project management experience working with commercial real estate projects in the United States and 2.5 years of experience in the international development industry working in Dubai, UAE, as a commercial real estate and software services project manager. Yin (2018) suggests limiting or eliminating any biases with a high level of transparency. I mitigated bias by cataloging a reflective journal of biases, feelings, and thoughts with hopes of understanding how they can influence the research (Watt, 2007). Beginner researchers use reflexivity to determine what they know and how they think they came to realize it (Watt, 2007). I am confident I mitigated bias by combining the interview protocol (see Appendix) and reflective journal methods. Researchers use an interview protocol to obtain generous, focused data that capture the participants' experiences (Castillo-Montoya, 2016).

As a certified project manager registered with PMI's global organization database, I have sworn to maintain the highest ethical and professional code of conduct. As a PMI member, I had sufficient access to field participants who are certified project managers who have taken the same oath. Per Walden University, I also followed the three basic ethical principles of the *Belmont Report*: (a) respect for persons, (b) beneficence, and (c) justice (National Commission for the Protection of Human Subjects and Biomedical and Behavioral Research, 1979). According to the *Belmont Report,* respect for persons is the requirement to acknowledge autonomy and the necessity to protect individuals with diminished autonomy. I demonstrated the utmost care to all participants. Beneficence is the requirement to treat persons ethically by respecting their decisions, protecting them from harm, and securing their well-being. Lastly, justice requires that all persons be treated equally with the accepted formulations, for example, individual need, individual effort, societal contribution, and merit. In compliance with *The Belmont Report,* I used an informed consent form to provide participants with the purpose of the interview and doctoral study and communicate their right to withdraw from the interview.

13

Participants

I determined a detailed set of eligibility criteria to generate accurate and productive results and findings. To be eligible, the doctoral study participants must have worked as project managers for an international development project located in the UAE. The participants should have at least 5 years of experience in the field and have proven success and challenges within the triple constraints of international development projects. Participants also needed to be certified PMP or in the process of gaining certification and be currently registered members with the PMI. PMI's (2017) Code of Ethics and Professional Conduct sets forth expectations of practitioners in the global project management community. It articulates the ideals that project managers aspire to and the mandatory behaviors they need to assume in their professional and volunteer roles. The Code of Ethics and Professional Conduct is vital in minimizing ethical concerns and avoiding unethical practices (Saunders et al., 2015). As project management experts currently working or volunteering in the field, the results and findings may be esoteric, furthering the doctoral study's validity.

To reach the eligible study participants, I relied on the PMI members page to search for project managers who meet eligibility criteria. I also connected with project managers from my LinkedIn connections list and professional group pages. Last, I gained access to various potential participants through the PMI UAE Khaleeji Chapter membership because of my former volunteer experience. To advance access to participants, I contacted the PMI UAE Khaleeji Chapter administrators via email and conveyed the purpose of the doctoral study. Upon receiving the chapter leader's approval, I asked the leadership team to choose an authorized representative to send out a communication to chapter members to invite them to participate in my study. I did not ask the PMI UAE Khaleeji chapter leaders to recruit study participants. The chapter communication included my personal contact information for interested participants to contact me without the chapter's inclusion. Therefore, once the participants' credentials meet the eligibility criteria and the participants agree to the study, I sent them an informed consent form via email.

Also, I established a working relationship with the study participants. I expounded on my academic and professional background during the initial contact with the study participants. I also explained how I created the research question and why I decided to pursue the research topic. DeJonckheere and Vaughn (2019) recommended researchers maintain an ethical attitude with respect, sensitivity, and tact from initiation. I considered power imbalances between myself and the research participants and not influence any relationships. Last, I maintained a high standard of professionalism by limiting personal information and experiences with research participants.

14

Research Method and Design

Research Method

The research method chosen for this doctoral study was the qualitative research method. Qualitative research is associated with an interpretive philosophy of the TOC (Saunders et al., 2015). Qualitative research is sometimes referred to as naturalistic because researchers need to operate within a natural setting to establish trust, participation, access to the participants' thought processes, and in-depth understandings (Saunders et al., 2015). Qualitative researchers receive a behind the scenes description of how participants feel and how other forces drive their experience (Korstjens & Moser, 2017). In the form of interview questions, data collection may alter and emerge during the research process, leading to increased data (Saunders et al., 2015).

As a qualitative researcher and experienced project manager, I believe that I understood what participants said, interacted effectively with participants, and analyzed the data and reported the findings accurately. Quantitative researchers use larger samples to quantify predefined outcomes generalized to a larger group versus qualitative studies focused on smaller models (Korstjens & Moser, 2017). Quantitative research methods are often structured, which would not have been an appropriate research method for this study. Also, testing a hypothesis was not the purpose of this study. Mixed-methods research is qualitative and quantitative and is used to verify the analytical procedure and if the hypothesis is true (Saunders et al., 2015). I did not use the quantitative method. Therefore, a mixed-methods approach was not appropriate.

Research Design

A multiple qualitative case study research design is an in-depth inquiry into a topic or phenomenon within its real-life setting to understand the study topic's dynamics (Saunders et al., 2015). Case study researchers facilitate multiple perspective analyses that provides a holistic understanding of cultural systems and insightful answers to exploratory questions (Basias & Pollalis, 2018). In contrast, an ethnography research design is the study of culture within a society, and researchers collect data through observations, interviews, and artifacts (Korstjens & Moser, 2017). Therefore, culture is not the business problem and is not an appropriate research design for this doctoral study. Researchers use the phenomenology research design to collect data via in-depth interviews sorted by experiences and themes (Korstjens & Moser, 2017). Experiential world views and their impact are not the data I need to collect; therefore, phenomenology is not the appropriate research design for this doctoral study. A qualitative multiple case study was the optimal choice design for my doctoral study because the data retrieved from the strategy described real-world issues within a real-life setting, which helped answer the research question.

To ensure proper data saturation, I used triangulation and member checking when conducting my interviews with my participants. The interviews were digitally audio-recorded utilizing the interview source website and transcribed verbatim to facilitate the data's reliability. As member checking happened, the researcher asked the participant additional questions if needed to confirm the accuracy and obtain any further information or potential correction of data (Birt et al., 2016; Spiers et al., 2018). Quigley and Simpson (2016) recommended that researchers distribute copies of the interview manuscript to participants to interpret more accurately. Researchers also conduct more in-depth member checking using real-time interview transcription and card sorts to inform the research (Madill & Sullivan, 2018). After the interview concluded, I provided the participants with a digital copy of the entire interview manuscript to verify the data and provide any additional information. I ensured that all information was interpreted correctly within the member checking phase and reached the data saturation point when no new themes surfaced.

15

Ethical Research

According to Saunders et al. (2015), the research quality depends on the researcher's integrity and objectivity. Therefore, the researcher's ethical responsibility is to be truthful accurate and avoid dishonesty with the data's data and results. Thus, the informed consent form was mandatory for all study participants. Saunders et al. stated the principle of informed consent involves researchers providing sufficient information and assurances about taking part to allow individuals to understand the implications of participation and to reach a fully informed decision about whether or not to do so with no pressure. The informed consent form prevented any form of harm towards the participants and ensured privacy and confidentiality. Participants had the opportunity to withdraw from the doctoral study at any time by simply emailing the researcher the request to remove. There were not any incentives given to the participants for consenting to the study.

I conducted my research virtually because I could travel to the UAE due to the global pandemic's socio-economic factors. The question of ethics arose from whether online communities used in research constitute public or private spaces (Roberts, 2015). Researchers should consider general public access, members' perception, community statements, topic sensitivity, and the online community's permanent records when making their initial assessments (Roberts, 2015). Walden University's IRB board confirmed and approved the use of online communities associated with this doctoral study before the research began, thus avoiding ethical issues and academic integrity. The IRB approval number is 08-20-21-0747829. Code numbering ensured that all study participants' identities or other identifying information were not in the study. I used codes such as P1 for participant 1, P2 for participant 2, and so forth.

Lastly, I securely filed all study participant data for 5 years with complete confidentiality protection. I stored interview transcripts, member checking documents, audio recordings, informed consent forms, interview protocol documents, video recordings, and other data in an encrypted, password-protected file accessed only by the researcher. At the end of the 5 years, I will properly destroy the data.

16

Data Collection Instruments

Primary data is collected for the researcher's specific research problem, backed by sources, using procedures fitting the research problem best (Boeije & Hox, 2005). As a researcher, I am the primary data collection instrument to discover the strategies project managers use to reduce the negative impact on the triple constraints of cost, schedule, and scope. I achieved the desired results by conducting virtual semistructured interviews with project managers employed in the international development industry in the UAE. Researchers who conduct semistructured interviews provide the opportunity to probe answers, where interviewees can explain and build on their responses leading towards more significance and depth to the obtained data (Saunders et al., 2015). Therefore, I used semistructured interviews to gain valuable data and answer the research question. Researchers are enabled to address a defined topic while allowing participants to answer truthfully, discussing issues and topics pertinent to their experiences using an interview schedule (Evans & Lewis, 2018). The interview protocol in the appendix was the defined schedule that I used to guide the interview and allow relevant themes to develop. Upon completing the interview, interview data were sorted into themes and analyzed.

I cross-checked the data received from the semistructured interviews by researching the participants' profiles online. According to Saunders et al. (2015), validity/credibility refers to the extent to which the researcher has gained access to a participants' knowledge and experience, inferring meanings the participant intends from the participants' language. Findings researchers derive from semistructured interviews are not necessarily meant to be repeatable since they reflect real-time experience at the time of collection and are subject to change (Saunders et al., 2015). Therefore, orchestrating research on the participants ensures the reliability and validity of the data. Transcripts from verbal interviews accurately recorded the data. The interview questions are listed in Section 1 of the doctoral study and the appendix. I ensured validity and credibility by conducting member checking and follow-up interviews to confirm the participants' transcripts and data points.

Besides interviews, I also reviewed existing documentation provided by project managers employed by UAE-based international development companies. Examples of documents included public records, materials extracted from the internet, and physical evidence (Hancock & Algozzine, 2017). I searched for lessons learned from the project managers to ensure their reliability, validity, and credibility. Project managers often have a log of lessons learned to improve similar future projects (PMI, 2017). Physical evidence includes anything physical associated with the case being reviewed, such as applications and tools used in international development project management and strategy (Hancock & Algozzine, 2017). The interviews provided ample information to identify what strategies project managers use to meet the triple constraints of international development projects' cost, schedule, and scope.

17

Data Collection Technique

According to Clark and Vealé (2018), qualitative researchers should record data without using numbers, such as opinions, feelings, and experiences. International development projects are unique projects; therefore, as the researcher, data collection and analysis was focused interpretive thinking (Clark & Vealé, 2018). Interpretive thinking allows the researcher to engage conscientiously in a subjective perception of the interviewee's experience (Clark & Vealé, 2018). The research question for this qualitative research study was "what are the strategies project managers use to meet the cost, schedule, and scope of international development projects?" I chose semistructured interviews as the data collection technique to answer the research question. The nature of the questions and the ensuing discussion means data will be captured by audio-recording the conversation while taking observation notes (Saunders et al., 2015). I conducted face-to-face video interviews utilizing Zoom to make the experience more personable and comfortable while observing their body language and responses. With the participants' permission, I recorded the semistructured interviews' audio and video to avoid misinterpretation and conduct thematic analysis. The interviews took up to 45 minutes to complete. Follow-up interviews took up to 30 minutes to complete. Upon completion of each interview, I transcribed the data. Researchers should begin data analysis immediately preceding transcription, so researchers become aware of emerging categories and themes as early in the research process as possible (Liljedahl et al., 2019). One advantage of using semistructured interviews as a data collection technique was researchers collected a large amount of data on usually small, purposeful samples (Boeije & Hox, 2005).

On the contrary, the disadvantage was obtaining a representative and accurate participant response. I have carefully designed the interview questions for more valuable answers to combat this disadvantage. I also conducted member checking of the participant's responses to ensure accuracy.

18

Data Organization Technique

Data was collected digitally utilizing audio recording, note-taking, and video recording with Zoom. I transcribed the semistructured interviews using Microsoft Word and then transferred the information into Microsoft Excel to sort and code. Clark and Vealé (2018) stated coding are an essential component a researcher can use to develop a sound qualitative analysis. When data is analyzed to decipher its core meaning, decoding occurs (Clark & Vealé, 2018). When the researcher labels the information with an appropriate code, the encoding occurs (Clark & Vealé, 2018). After sorting and coding the data in Microsoft Excel, I reviewed the codes for patterns and common themes. I continued to review the data, searched for various themes, and developed more themes as additional findings were presented until data was saturated.

Throughout the data collection and analysis process, I kept a reflective journal to examine and reflect on the participants' answers and the data elicited. I analyzed my role in collecting and interpreting the data and reflected on my pre-conceived assumptions. By creating a reflective journal, researchers provide a secondary analysis that supports an alternative interpretation of the qualitative research and overall scientific progress (Feldman & Shaw, 2019). Researchers should engage in a subjective perception of another person's experience to interpret the data with minimal bias and personal beliefs to represent the topic (Clark & Vealé, 2018). To ensure the participants' confidentiality and privacy, I applied unique identifiers using alphanumeric codes such as P1 for participant 1, P2 for participant 2, etc. I electronically stored the data on a password-protected Excel file for 5 years. The file will be stored on an external hard disk and locked in a safe in the researcher's home. Researchers can use archived qualitative research data to contribute to the reliability and generalization of findings, secondary analysis, research methods exploration, and critique (Feldman & Shaw, 2019). After 5 years, I will destroy the data file.

19

Data Analysis

Triangulation involves using more than one data source and collection method to confirm the validity, credibility, and authenticity of research data, analysis, and interpretation (Saunders et al., 2015). For qualitative research, triangulation adds depth to the data collection serving as a link between triangulation and data saturation, mitigating one's bias (Fusch et al., 2018). Triangulation in qualitative research began in the 1970s when Denzin formulated a more systematic approach suggesting four forms of triangulation, theoretical, investigator, data, and methodological (Flick, 2018). I have chosen the methodological triangulation approach. Researchers conduct methodological triangulation by combining various techniques in one study (Korstjens & Moser, 2017). My chosen instruments and techniques are semistructured interviews, observation notes, and business documentation.

Based on the documents, observation notes, and audio/video recordings of the interviews, I chose the within-method tri-

76

angulation. The within-method triangulation process allows researchers to combine questions and narratives for more specific findings and an episodic view (Flick, 2018). By gathering and organizing the participants' human experiences, I grouped the emerging themes. I triangulated the data by first focusing on the meaning of a phenomenon from a subjective perspective. Second, I triangulated the data from an interpretive perspective. I then contextualized the participants' statements.

Researchers conduct thematic analysis by identifying patterns and themes within the data (Evans & Lewis, 2018). After I completed each interview, the process of thematic analysis began. According to Yin (2018), there are five steps to data analysis; (a) compiling, (b) disassembling, (c) reassembling, (d) interpreting, and (e) concluding. First, I completed the compiling phase by transcribing the interview. I gathered my observation notes and completed comparison with the transcriptions, noting any additional concepts. Next, I disassembled by re-reading the transcriptions and notes and searched for critical ideas, themes, and patterns. The theme should capture relevancy towards the research question, reproach the theoretical position, and frequently appear within the dataset (Evans & Lewis, 2018). I reassembled all theme data in chronological order in an Excel spreadsheet. Once I gathered the data from each interview, I interpreted the critical themes with documentary evidence, related to the conceptual framework, and organized them alphabetically. I then began to cluster the themes for all the interviews and correlated them with the literature review, the most current literature, and the conceptual framework. Lastly, I concluded the analysis and summarized my findings with recommendations for future research and generalized broader research.

78

20

Reliability and Validity

Reliability

According to Spiers et al. (2018), reliability in qualitative research is rooted in the idea of data adequacy, showing consistent support for the researcher's analysis across study participants. Leung (2015) stated reliability is embedded inconsistency, achieved with data comparison and accuracy verification through data triangulation. I ensured consistency throughout my study by coding, analyzing, and interpreting all data. By recording all changes, I produced a reliable, dependable account of the emerging research focus, easily replicated and understood by others (Saunders et al., 2015).

Dependability

Trochim (2020) stated the idea of dependability emphasizes the need for the researcher to account for the changes during the research process. I enhanced my study's dependability by first member checking the data. All interview transcripts sent back to participants for feedback and review is the process of member checking (Korstjens & Moser, 2017). In the interview protocol located in the appendix, I scheduled the member checking interview first. Then upon completion of synthesis of the interview transcription, I asked the participant follow-up questions. Any corrections made to interpret data with final confirmation of the interview results further the study's dependability (Korstjens & Moser, 2017). Therefore, I included a record confirmation of the interview results. According to Trochim, reaching data saturation will also help ensure dependability in the research findings and the ever-changing context within which the research.

Validity

Validity in qualitative research refers to the appropriateness of the tools, processes, and data, according to Leung (2015). In parallel to credibility, internal validity is used to ensure that the research participants' representations match what they intended (Saunders et al., 2015). Some researchers refrain from the term validity and instead assert that verisimilitude, reality-aligned analysis, is more appropriate (Johnson & Rose, 2020). Albeit validity or realism, I demonstrated validity by organizing themes and interpretations, making a change in people's lives with the research by confirming credibility, addressing transferability and confirmability, and ensuring data saturation.

Credibility

Researchers achieve credibility when qualitative research results are credible from the participant's perspective (Trochim, 2020). Yin (2015) stated a credible study provides assurance the researcher has properly collected and interpreted the data, so the conclusions accurately reflect the world studied. Member checking of the analyzed data, participant transcript review, triangulation, and interview protocol are also forms of credibility. To improve the most accurate recall chances, I completed the member checking process within 7 days of the interview. Once I transcribed the interview, I presented the transcription to the participants to ensure the notes were as accurate as possible and represented their views.

Transferability

Trochim (2020) stated in qualitative research; transferability is the ability for a study's results to be generalized or reproducible with the different contexts of your research, such as a smaller/larger sample size or an alternate location. Researchers ensure transferability by thoroughly describing the research context and assumptions. Other researchers wishing to transfer the results to a different setting will then be responsible for judging the transfer's sense (Trochim, 2020). I ensured that the study's conclusions could be transferred to other studies regardless of populations, settings, or time.

Confirmability

The degree to which others could confirm or corroborate the results is considered confirmability (Trochim, 2020). To enhance the study's confirmability, I documented the procedures for checking and rechecking the data via member checking. I also reported and described any negative instances contradicting my previous observations. As a researcher, it is my responsibility to be as transparent as possible throughout the research process, being objective and unbiased (Trochim, 2020). Therefore, I maintained all raw data, findings, results, etc., available for 5 years. After 5 years, I will destroy all documents. Triangulation applied throughout the study strengthens the credibility of a study (Yin, 2015). Fusch et al. (2018) argued triangulation occurs when the data is accurate and truthful. Inferences can link back to the conceptual framework. Since my research included semistructured, virtual interviews, I took notes during the interview observing the participants for nonverbal cues and body language. Member checking of the interview responses combined with my notes and audio recordings enabled me to triangulate the data and improve this study's validity.

Data Saturation

While triangulation adds depth to the collected data, the more in-depth the data, the more the data's saturation (Fusch et al., 2018). As the researcher, I ensured data saturation when I no longer received new information, themes, codes, or patterns. The semistructured interviews I conducted were an essential tool to collect data from various participants' perspectives. I continued to probe with follow-up questions to gain additional insight into the participants' experience until no new data emerged.

83

21

Transition and Summary

In section 2 of the study, I began with the purpose statement's reiteration and my role as the researcher. I then described the participants and their respective eligibility requirements. Next, I expanded on the nature of the study within the research method and research design, clearly identifying how I will ultimately ensure data saturation. The researcher explains the scope of the study defined in the population and sampling sections. Then, I expanded on how I plan to research ethically collect data with specific instruments. Lastly, I discussed the reliability and validity of the study. In section 3 of the study, I will first present the findings. Next, I will discuss the application to professional practice, implications for social change, recommendations for action, and further research recommendations. Lastly, I will discuss my reflections and conclude the doctoral study.

III

Application to Professional Practice and Implications for Change

22

Introduction

The purpose of this qualitative multiple case study was to explore the strategies project managers use to meet international development projects' triple constraints of cost, schedule, and scope. To answer the research question, I interviewed five project managers with at least 5 years' experience working as a project manager in the UAE. The interviewees were members of the PMI and had obtained the organization's PMP certification or were pursuing it. I conducted semistructured virtual interviews using Zoom. The findings revealed the participating project managers' methods to meet projects' triple constraints of cost, schedule, and scope. I identified three themes from the participants' responses to the interview questions. The three themes were (a) scope management, (b) stakeholder management, and (c) project management planning. In Section 3, I present the findings and consider their applications for professional practice and implications for social change. Last, I offer recommendations for action and future research, reflect on my research, and provide a conclusion to the study.

23

Presentation of the Findings

The overarching research question that I sought to answer was, What strategies do project managers use to meet the cost, schedule, and scope of international development projects? I conducted five virtual interviews on Zoom of project managers with at least 5 years' experience working in the UAE on international development projects. All five participants agreed to audio and video recordings of their interview, followed by member checking sessions. I transcribed the interviews, prepared a summary, and shared the data with each participant. The participants confirmed the data as correct and did not provide new data or documentation of lessons learned, indicating that I had reached data saturation.

Three themes emerged from analyzing the participants' responses to the interview questions. The themes highlight strategies that project managers use to reduce the negative impact on the triple constraints of cost, schedule, and scope. The three themes are

- scope management,

- stakeholder management, and
- project management planning.

These three themes were the most mentioned responses from all participants, as shown in Table 2. The table shows the codes and themes associated with each interview question. The participants associated with each code are also shown for each interview question.

Table 2

Summary of Qualitative Thematic Analysis

Question	Code	Theme	Participant data
Q1	A, B, C, D, E, F	Lessons learned documentation (A), scope (B)	A - P1 B - P2, P3, P4, P5
Q2	B, G, H, I, J, K	Scope, quality (G), project planning (H), change management (I), stakeholder (J), foreign culture (K)	B - P1, P2, P4 G - P2, P4, P5 H - P3, P4 I, J - P3 K - P5
Q3	B, J, E, L, M, I	Scope, stakeholder, change management	B - P1, P3, P4, P5 J - P1 I - P3, P4
Q4	N, H, O, K, P, J	Resources (N), project planning, foreign culture, stakeholder	N - P1, P4, P5 H - P1 K - P2, P3, P5 J - P3, P5
Q5	Q, J, R, S	Communications (Q), stakeholder	Q – All Ps J - P2, P3, P4
Q6	T, U, V, H, J, B, I, K, Q, N, W, R, A	Project planning, stakeholder, scope, change management, foreign culture, communications, resources	H - P2, P3 J, B, I - P3 K, N - P4 A - P5
Q7	T, U, V, H, A, X	Project planning, lessons learned documentation	H - P2 A - P3, P4
Q8	N/A	N/A	N/A
Q9	Y, Z, Z1, J, B, H, Z2, A, Z3, G, N, W	Stakeholder, scope, project planning, quality, resources	J, H - P2 B - P2, P4 A - P3 G, N - P5

Summary of Qualitative Thematic Analysis

Note. Q = interview question; P = participant. Q1 refers to Interview Question 1 and P1, Participant 1. Themes listed in the code column are labeled with the letters A through Z, with additional themes marked as Z1, Z2, and Z3. I highlighted the themes with six or more mentions in the theme and participant data columns. Question 8 asked for the participants' knowledge of the TOC and, therefore, did not produce strategic themes.

24

Theme 1: Scope Management

The first theme from the data analysis was the use of a scope management plan to reduce the negative impact on the triple constraints of cost, schedule, and scope. The interviewees' responses confirm the findings of PMI's scope management process to ensure that a project includes all the necessary and required work to complete the project within the determined budget and schedule (PMI, 2017). All participants noted that project requirements must be clearly defined at the planning phase to eliminate or reduce any changes to the scope later. Changes made later in the project cause adverse effects to cost and schedule.

P1 discussed how scope changes caused one of their projects at Company 1 to exceed their budget due to legal authorities in the region not approving the design and developer requirements, although local government authorities did approve. P1 advised that project managers need to be cautious and aware of scope based on the country's limits. P4 described a similar situation as scope creep and recommended change control management while working on a project at Company

4. P5 discussed how their government clients provided a broad scope where "requirements were taken very lightly," and the project ended in a considerable loss. P1, P4, and P5 described viewpoints that align with Molenaar et al.'s (2019) statement that project managers do not share the excessive scope or quality buffers detected in the specifications with the client. P2 discussed providing a 20% buffer to manage changes in requirements, thus reducing the impact to timeline and cost.

Vereijssen et al. (2017) stated that project managers need to understand the problem from different angles and be inclusive of stakeholder diversity. P1 said their past project failed to meet their quality goals due to the stakeholders' unclear scope. P2 discussed how the scope requirements in one of their projects were 95% factored in; however, the client added a requirement that altered the scope. P2 understood the business needs and the relationship between the business and stakeholders and made the changes. P3 established the needs and identified the right stakeholders in the planning stages of their project. P3 stated,

What really matters is if the outcomes are realized ahead of time, then you will have more success if the outcomes are well established, and you have the right engagement with the stakeholders, then project delivery will not be negatively impacted," which aligns with Vereijssen et al.'s research.

Strategies are needed for project managers to reduce the negative impact on the triple constraints of cost, schedule, and scope.

Collect and Define Requirements, Then Control the Scope in Detail

All five participants described the importance of collecting all the requirements in detail from the very beginning of the project. The critical difference in collecting the requirements from the standard project management process is to clearly communicate the exact needs from the stakeholders and realize the outcomes ahead of time. The outcomes need to be well established with the proper engagement of stakeholders. The requirements need to be clearly articulated by the stakeholders, and the project manager must ensure they are providing this information. Once the client and stakeholders express their needs, the project manager can clearly define the scope. The project manager must communicate with the clients and stakeholders and control changes. The level of effort to accept any changes and their impact on cost, schedule, and quality will impact acceptance. Project managers will often provide a change management plan. P5 described freezing the scope, and any changes would need to be considered an enhancement. P2 incorporated a 20% cost buffer to cover additional requirements. Again, if all requirements are captured by the project team early on, scope changes will not be needed later.

Educate Yourself on Environmental Factors

Global project managers working on international development projects may have legal and regulatory issues that arise. Governmental agency delays can be catastrophic to an international development project. A key strategy is to review lessons learned from previous projects and regulatory agency policies and procedures. Project managers need to be aware of the levels of approval necessary from government agencies that can hinder progress and or project closure. Also, project managers need to be mindful of material quality from different countries of origin. The project manager may not choose to procure a cheaper material; however, they cannot sacrifice the quality. The project managers must choose quality over quantity, being mindful of possible supply chain issues.

Relationship to Conceptual Framework

Scope management aligns with the TOC used by project managers to reduce the negative impact on the triple constraints of cost, schedule, and scope of an international development project. Project managers view the TOC thinking processes as a problem-solving method that offers win-win solutions (Cox & Schleier, 2010; Lacerda et al., 2014). P1 agreed the TOC assisted in identifying schedule constraints, whereas P2 argued the TOC 5FS should identify more than the triple constraints by adding quality. P3 also agreed the TOC helps focus on issues and is relatable to other projects outside of operations. P4 advised the TOC helps to identify risks and scheduling issues solely, whereas P5 did not find the TOC helpful with their projects. According to Stratton and Yeong (2017), project managers use TOC S&T trees to create and implement change. All the participants agreed they use a change management tool to address changes most strategically and measurably.

25

Theme 2: Stakeholder Management

The second theme from the data analysis was project managers' use of a stakeholder management strategy to reduce the negative impact on the triple constraints of cost, schedule, and scope. The interviewees' responses confirm the findings of PMI's stakeholder management process. According to the *PMBOK*, the ability of the project manager and team to identify and appropriately engage all stakeholders can mean the difference between project success and failure (PMI, 2017).

Responsible project managers, leaders, and stakeholders transform the decision-making process to improve project outcomes. All participants agreed clear communication is necessary with stakeholders. P2 created a steering committee of leadership and stakeholders to communicate for help, which improved the overall project outcome during their employment at Company 2. P2 and P3 expressed similar viewpoints to Batista et al. (2019), who argued that beyond strategy, operations, and projects, the stakeholders should be included as one of the bases for competitive advantage. P3 stated that project managers need to advise stakeholders on the level of effort, possible changes, and the support required to manage change. P3 and P5 both reported experiencing schedule delays due to local government challenges. While working at Company 5, P5 dealt with multiple stakeholders from multiple countries, limited resources, and low-quality materials, causing project delays. P3's project changed leadership and had government approval delays for 18 months. All participants agreed that some issues are out of one's control; however, over time, one can build trustworthy relationships with government and leadership stakeholders to better prepare. Strategies are needed for project managers to reduce the negative impact on the triple constraints of cost, schedule, and scope.

Identify Key Stakeholders, Build the Relationship, and Prepare for Culture Differences

All five participants worked on international development projects with diverse teams from multiple countries. Global project managers must be human-oriented and relationship-oriented, building trustworthy relationships with local government, industry, and authorities (Aarseth et al., 2014; Ciric et al., 2019; Haaskjold et al., 2019; Nevstad et al., 2021; Pirju, 2018). The participants recommended the strategy of identifying key stakeholders beyond the client. Key stakeholders are government authorities, industry experts, and company leadership. Project managers should develop a business relationship with the key stakeholders, increasing the likelihood of more minor constraint issues (Díaz-Barcos et al., 2020). The study participants explained global project managers need to be aware of cultural differences when working on international development projects. For example, P3 stated "depending on the country; the experience will be different adapting to their cultures; some countries are very relaxed and take their time with decision-making while other cultures value speed and accuracy." Project managers should recognize these cultural differences and manage the stakeholder relationship accordingly with team building strategies and effective engagement (Eweje et al., 2021; Kozhakhmetova et al., 2019).

Clear Communications and Project Status Transparency Are Paramount

Global project managers need to recognize differences in culture and engage with different people. P4 described a project with Company 4 where no one spoke English and Google translate had to be used in the meetings. P2 stated some stakeholders do not understand project management. As project managers, it is our responsibility to communicate our process, making stakeholders realize the effects of scope changes and the impact on the other constraints, levels of effort involved with changes, and its implications to business value. All participants explained the importance of complete transparency throughout the project. Project managers need to address any challenges at the onset of the project. Project managers should share both positive and negative feedback with the project team in feedback loops. Collective sharing of feedback encourages personal development and effective project management learning (Yap et al., 2018).

Relationship to Conceptual Framework

Stakeholder management aligns with the TOC used by project managers to reduce the negative impact on the triple constraints of cost, schedule, and scope of an international development project. Specifically, the implementation of CCPM guided companies to streamline project management processes and improve communication between the company and its stakeholders (Dostatni & Trojanowska, 2017). Although the participants did not utilize CCPM, their thought processes and stakeholder management experiences are similar in this regard.

26

Theme 3: Project Planning

The third theme from the data analysis was project managers utilized a project management planning strategy to reduce the negative impact on the triple constraints of cost, schedule, and scope. According to PMI (2017), the project management planning process consists of establishing the total scope of the effort, defining objectives, and developing the course of action required to attain those objectives. The project management plan defines, prepares, and coordinates all plan components (PMI, 2017). The interviewees' responses confirm the findings of PMI and Annany et al. (2018), stating project management exploited as a strategy of management skills, knowledge, and tools will lead to project success.

Due to poor project planning, all participants experienced negative impacts on cost, schedule, and scope. P1 explained project managers must plan for possible supply chain issues, natural disasters, war, and other common resource problems within international development projects. Project managers can reduce negative results by identifying problems well in advance (Díaz-Barcos et al., 2020). P1 explained at Company 1 the company focuses on doing things right, which includes creating a detailed project management plan, defining scope requirements accurately, gaining leadership buy-in and guidance, and focusing on process improvement with new technologies. Company 1's leadership teams take the extra step toward caring about the industry through knowledge sharing with other industry leaders. P2 and P3 argued excellent planning combined with clear communication and lessons learned documentation would help project managers succeed in projects which aligns directly with Fernandes et al.'s (2019) research. Fernandes et al. (2019) stated project managers would achieve better results when they strongly link planning practices to the combination of project management process groups. P3 noted at Company 3, the project managers felt they did not invest enough time to transition the project over once they completed their jobs. Poor transition planning from the project manager can also lead to project failure. Project managers need to invest in proper transitioning and handover to the right stakeholders and clients, ensuring updated project management planning and lessons learned documentation. The following two strategies provide a detailed overview of project managers' approaches in project management planning. Strategies are needed for project managers to reduce the negative impact on the triple constraints of cost, schedule, and scope.

Take as Much Time as Needed to Plan Correctly

Each participant discussed the need to take enough time to plan all project elements. P2 divided and conquered the activities and schedule by creating a good set of deliverables. Project managers should provide excellent planning in combination with communication. Project managers should check daily activities and provide status meetings daily or weekly as part of the project management planning process.

Create a Transition Plan With a Focus on Process Improvement

Global project managers must create a transition plan focusing on process improvement. P3 picked 10 projects from the past year and discussed what went well and what went wrong. Stakeholders provided feedback and dissected the projects to realize moments of failure. Project managers create lessons learned documents from the transition planning meetings for future knowledge sharing. P5 described taking these lessons learned and transition plans to industry leaders to help develop best practices within similar international development projects.

Relationship to Conceptual Framework

Project management planning aligns with the TOC used by project managers to reduce the negative impact on the triple constraints of cost, schedule, and scope of an international development project. Isharyanto et al. (2015) stated there is clear evidence the poor success rate of projects is due in part to poorly managed resources and recognition of constraints.

Therefore, the TOC can evaluate these issues and develop a breakthrough solution. Incorporating the TOC early in the planning phases of projects will reduce delays and keep projects within budget and scope.

27

Applications to Professional Practice

Reduced negative impacts on the triple constraints of cost, schedule, and scope resulted from the practical usage of scope management strategies by project managers of international development projects. Global development project managers that worked on international development projects utilized scope management strategies to define, validate, and control the scope with a clear focus on collecting all requirements initially. Project management standards and guidelines alone would not automatically lead to a positive impact on the triple constraints (Donnelly & Ika, 2017; Ika et al., 2020; Ika & Munro, 2020). Based on the study data, scope changes are the primary reason international development project managers do not meet their cost, schedule, and quality-related goals. Project managers captured requirements in detail to accurately encapsulate the project's scope. Feedback requests provided by the stakeholders are also captured before project commitment, enhancing scope definition. Project managers communicating the level of effort for scope changes while building trust and a relationship with the client/stakeholder also lead to positive outcomes. International development project managers must also be mindful of the government approvals and other country limitations that may impact the scope of work. The findings of this study might benefit international development project managers to reduce the negative impact on the triple constraints of cost, schedule, and scope using scope management strategies. Project managers' application of these findings might improve their scope management strategies.

Reduced negative impacts on the triple constraints of cost, schedule, and scope resulted from the practical usage of stakeholder management strategies by project managers of international development projects. Global development project managers utilized stakeholder management strategies to identify and engage all stakeholders appropriately to increase the chances of project success of their international development projects. Planning stakeholder engagement is developing approaches to involve stakeholders based on their needs, expectations, interests, location, and potential impact on the project (PMI, 2017). Project managers developed business relationships with stakeholders to focus on engagement, goals, and issues while noticing stakeholder behavior. Project managers recognized and adjusted planning due to cultural differences during their international development projects. Some projects included stakeholders from multiple countries and government agencies, and therefore, project managers developed thorough stakeholder and communication management plans. Project managers communicated to stakeholders their change management protocols and identified the business needs of their clients. Project managers recommended complete transparency shared delays and impacts on changes, so stakeholders have a clear understanding. The key is not to lead the project in isolation but to lead the project vocally, engaging with everyone and adapting to different cultures. In addition, project managers reskilled their workforce with legal and regulatory compliance knowledge. The findings of this study might benefit international development project managers to reduce the negative impact on the triple constraints of cost, schedule, and scope using stakeholder management strategies. Project managers' application of these findings might improve their stakeholder management strategies.

Reduced negative impacts on the triple constraints of cost, schedule, and scope resulted from the practical usage of project management planning strategies by project managers of international development projects. Global development project managers utilized project management planning strategies to establish the total scope of effort, define objectives, and develop a course of action to increase the chances of project success of their international development projects. Project managers executed the project only after reviewing the scope requirements, risks, constraints, and quality, creating a complete project management plan once stakeholders provided input. Starting with limited knowledge and not allocating enough time to plan leads to rework of deliverables, which increases cost, delays in schedule, and scope changes. Multi-million-dollar international development project managers created smaller sub-plans, dividing and conquering the scheduled activities and monitoring them with clear communications. Project managers added budget contingency plans and buffers in preparation for future scope changes, resources, and supply chain issues. Meetings are held by project managers and stakeholders weekly in-person and remotely, and project managers check activities daily, identifying any problems and addressing them urgently. Project managers logged meeting minutes in lessons learned documentation and saved them for future review and knowledge sharing. The findings of this study might benefit international development project managers to reduce the negative impact on the triple constraints of cost, schedule, and scope using project management planning strategies. Project managers' application of these findings might improve their project management planning strategies.

28

Implications for Social Change

PMI research indicates the construction sector has one of the most significant gaps between current and projected jobs in project management-oriented employment (PMI, 2022). The employment growth rate is 13.2% higher overall; however, training new project managers will take time (PMI, 2022). PMI researchers predict the global economy will need 25 million new project professionals by 2030 (PMI, 2022). Project managers have found ways to facilitate cross-border projects through remote collaboration and knowledge sharing, as shown in this study. The use of more innovative and creative project management strategies reduces adverse effects to the triple constraints of cost, schedule, and scope, increasing business profitability and contributing to a healthier, safer work environment. The implementation of scope, stakeholder, and project management planning strategies by international development project managers may be a way to elevate the project management industry for improving social change and cultural differences, thus benefiting society. Project managers might use the findings of this study to implement scope, stakeholder, and project management planning strategies that result in a greater social consciousness of the project management community and their international development projects' success.

29

Recommendations for Action

The purpose of this qualitative multiple case study was to discover what strategies project managers use to reduce the negative impact on an international development project's triple constraint of cost, schedule, and scope. I recommend that project managers use the findings of this study to be cognizant of the benefits of imposing scope, stakeholder, and project management planning strategies to reduce the negative impact on the triple constraints. I recommend project managers focus on scope change management, better communication between stakeholders and regulatory agencies, and planning excellence.

My goal is to publish the results of this study and share the findings with other project management professionals. First, I will share the findings with the study participants. Second, I intend to submit articles for consideration in peer-reviewed journals such as the *International Journal of Project Management*. Finally, I will pursue speaking engagements to present the study's findings at conferences and webinars

offered by professional organizations such as the PMI and
TOCPA, which is the Theory of Constraints Practitioners
Alliance.

30

Recommendations for Further Research

Apotential limitation of this study was the participants' unwillingness to share adverse outcomes of their projects. This limitation was not realized. In the interviews, participants were more than willing to discuss adverse project outcomes within their firms but did not share their lessons learned documentation. I recommend future researchers attempt to collect this information as well. Each participant resided and worked for firms based in the UAE. I recommend future researchers explore other geographical locations and conduct qualitative research on what strategies project managers managing international development projects are using to reduce the negative impact on the triple constraints of cost, schedule, and scope. One strategy mentioned during the interviews was implementing an incentive bonus program for completing milestone stages to help motivate the project team. Future researchers may want to explore whether incentive programs are a successful strategy to reduce the negative impact on the triple constraints of cost, schedule, and scope and what implications, if any, these programs have for quality.

31

Reflections

I have 20 years of experience working as a project manager with 6 years of experience working internationally on global strategic projects. In reviewing of the academic literature, I discovered new research and project management professionals addressing international development project challenges. During the interview process, I expected project managers to discuss their project management strategies, which they did. Still, I gained additional insight and a new perspective into international development project management struggles and how to address those struggles more effectively. I am an avid believer in ongoing personal development, and the process of completing this doctoral study contributed to this belief. I realized I must approach each international development project differently and mold project management strategies to adapt to the elements of those specific projects. The complexity of international development projects drives project managers to constantly evolve and elevate themselves with continuous education and knowledge sharing within the industry. After speaking with the study participants, we all shared this sentiment which leads me to believe the project management industry and community are transforming into a community of thought leaders passionate for improvement and social change. I was able to gain information without bias, remaining neutral throughout the data collection and analysis process. I hope with the information shared in this study, those project managers who work locally and globally will incorporate the valuable findings into their everyday work because I will surely do so.

32

Conclusion

International development projects were more likely to fail without project managers successfully implementing scope, stakeholder, and project management planning strategies. While working in globalized economies, project managers are constantly bombarded with issues often not scoped or planned into the project, thus forcing adaptation, quick thinking, and creativity with a solid project management foundation. Having a solid project management foundation is the key to the emerged themes. International development project managers develop a deep understanding of global trends affecting their project constraints of cost, schedule, and scope and create strategies to embrace and overcome them. As project managers continue to invest in furthering their project management education and knowledge sharing within the industry, project success rates will continue to increase. Project managers will also contribute to society, becoming changemakers setting themselves apart from organizational leadership while building an essential skillset. Project managers could use this study's recommendations and findings to enhance and refine their thought processes and execution of international development projects. This study's academic research and findings will provide project managers with the tools and techniques to mold their project management knowledge and implement real-world solutions to their challenges.

33

References

Aarseth, W., Rolstadås, A., & Andersen, B. (2014). Managing organizational challenges in global projects. *International Journal of Managing Projects in Business, 7*(1), 103–132. https://doi.org/10.1108/IJMPB-02-2011-0008

Acar, O. A., Tarakci, M., & van Knippenberg, D. (2018). Creativity and innovation under constraints: A cross-disciplinary integrative review. *Journal of Management, 45*(1), 96121. https://doi.org/10.1177/0149206318805832

Ahmed, S. (2019). A review on using opportunities of augmented reality and virtual reality in construction project management. *Organization, Technology and Management in Construction: An International Journal, 11*(1), 1839–1852. https://doi.org/10.2478/otmcj-2018-0012

Ahsan, K., & Kumar, P. (2018). Procurement issues in donor-funded international development projects. *Journal of Management in Engineering, 34*(6), Article 04018041. https://doi.org/10.1061/(ASCE)ME.1943-5479.0000648

Al Nahyan, M. T., Sohal, A. S., Hawas, Y. E., & Fildes,

B.(2014). Project management, infrastructure development and stakeholder engagement: A case study from the UAE. *Procedia Technology, 16*, 988991. https://doi.org/10.1016/j.protcy.2014.10.052

Alashwal, A. M., Fareed, N. F., & Al-obaidi, K. M. (2017). Determining success criteria and success factors for international construction projects for Malaysian contractors. *Construction Economics and Building, 17*(2), 6280. https://doi.org/10.5130/AJCEB.v17i2.5319

Al Nahyan, M. T., Sohal, A., Hawas, Y., & Fildes, B. (2019). Communication, coordination, decision-making and knowledge sharing: A case study in construction management. *Journal of Knowledge Management. 23*(9), 17641781. https://doi.org/10.1108/JKM-08-2018-0503

Al Nahyan, M., Fildes, B., Hawas, Y. E., & Sohal, A. S. (2019). Infrastructure development in the UAE: Communication and coordination issues amongst key stakeholders. In *Risk Management in Engineering and Construction* (1st ed.), 23. Routledge.

Al Nahyan, M., Hawas, Y. E., & Raza, M. (2021). An exploratory study of relationships between stakeholders' risk perceptions and their roles and experience in construction industry. *International Journal of Construction Management, 21*(7), 738–754. https://doi.org/10.1080/15623599.2019.1580833

Al-Rubaiei, Q., Musa, S., & Nifa, F. (2018). Project scope management through multiple
perspectives: A critical review of concepts. In *AIP Conference Proceedings, 2016*(1), 020025. AIP Publishing LLC.

Álvarez-Pérez, M., Pellicer, E., & Soler, M. (2018). Target value design: A different way
of approaching the constructive process in Spain. *Journal of*

Modern Project Management, 50–55. https://www.researchgate.net/publication/322644101_TARGET_VALUE_DESIGN_A_different_way_of_approaching_the_constructive_process_in_Spain

Ameyaw, E., Chan, A., DeGraft, O, Owusu, E., & Robert, O. (2019). Contemporary review of anti-corruption measures in construction project management. *Project Management Journal,* *50*(1), 40–56. https://doi.org/10.1177/8756972818808983

Anholon, R., Coelho, J., Novaski, O., Ordoñez, R., & Vanhoucke, M. (2019). A study of the critical chain project management method applied to a multi project system. *Project Management Journal,* *50*(3), 322–334. https://doi.org/10.1177/8756972819832203

Annany, Y., Keshk, A., & Maarouf, I. (2018). Special studies in management of construction project risks, risk concept, plan building, risk quantitative and qualitative analysis, risk response strategies. *Alexandria Engineering Journal, 57,* 3179–3187. https://doi.org/10.1016/j.aej.2017.12.003

Armenia, S.; Dangelico, R., Nonino, F., & Pompei, A. (2019). Sustainable project management: A conceptualization-oriented review and a framework proposal for future studies. *Sustainability, 11*(9), 22664. https://doi.org/10.3390/su11092664

Auclair, I., & Brière, S. (2020). Toward gendered projects in international development: Paradoxes, resistance and convergent approaches. *International Journal of Project Management, 38*(8), 500–514. https://doi.org/10.1016/j.ijproman.2020.07.004

Ballesteros-Sánchez, L., Ortiz-Marcos, I., Rodríguez-Rivero, R., & Romero, J. (2020). Finding the links between risk management and project success: Evidence from international development projects in Colombia. *Sustainability, 12*(21), 9294. https://doi.org/10.3390/su12219294

Banerjee, D., & Lowalekar, H. (2021). Communicating for change: A systems thinking approach. *Journal of Organizational Change Management, 34*(5), 1018–1035. https://doi.org/10.1108/JOCM-10-2020-0325

Banker, R., Byzalov, D., Fang, S., & Liang, Y. (2018). Cost management research. *Journal of Management Accounting Research, 30*(3), 187-209. https://doi.org/10.2308/jmar-51965

Barnett, J., Thorpe, S., Vasileiou, K., & Young, T. (2018). Characterizing and justifying sample size sufficiency in interview-based studies: Systematic analysis of qualitative health research over a 15-year period. *BMC Med Res Methodology, 18*, 148. https://doi.org/10.1186/s12874-018-0594-7

Basias, N., & Pollalis, Y. (2018). Quantitative and qualitative research in business & technology: Justifying a suitable research methodology. *Review of Integrative Business and Economics Research, 7*(1), 91–105. https://buscompress.com/journal-home.html

Batista, H. M., Ferreira, S., & Neto, J. (2019). Critical success factors on project and process management in competitive strategy implementation. *Brazilian Journal of Operations & Production Management, 16*(4), 605–616. https://doi.org/10.14488/BJOPM.2019.v16.n4.a6

Bauer, J., Sellitto, M., Souza, M., Vaccaro, G., & Vargas, A. (2019). The thinking process of the theory of constraints applied to public healthcare. *Business Process Management Journal, 25*(7), 1543–1563. https://doi.org/10.1108/BPMJ-06-2016-0118

Berner, M., Frattini, F., Latilla, V., & Petruzzelli, A. (2018).

Knowledge management, knowledge transfer, and organizational performance in the arts and crafts industry: A literature review. *Journal of Knowledge Management, 22*(6), 1310–1331. https://doi.org/10.1108/JKM-08-2017-0367

Bhandarkar, B., Narvel, Y., & Rane, S. (2020). Developing strategies to improve agility in the project procurement management (PPM) process. *Business Process Management Journal, 26*(1), 257–286. https://doi.org/10.1108/BPMJ-07-2017-0196

Birt, L., Cavers, D., Campbell, C., Scott, S., & Walter, F. (2016). Member checking: A tool to enhance trustworthiness or merely a nod to validation. *Qualitative Health Research, 26*(13), 1802–1811. https://doi.org/f8848w

Boeije, H., & Hox, J. (2005). Data collection, primary vs. secondary. *Encyclopedia of Social Measurement, 1*, 593–599.

Briére, S., & Proulx, D. (2013). The success of an international development project: Lessons drawn from a case between Morocco and Canada. *International Review of Administrative Sciences, 79*(1), 165–186. https://doi.org/10.1177/0020852312467620

Callistus, T., & Clinton, A. (2018). The role of monitoring and evaluation in construction project management. In *International Conference on Intelligent Human Systems Integration,* 571–582. Springer.

Cantarelli, C., & Genovese, A. (2021). Innovation potential of megaprojects: A systematic literature review. *Production Planning & Control,* 1–21. https://doi.org/10.1080/09537287.2021.2011462

Carral, L., Diaz, E., Fraguela, J., Iglesias, G., & San Cristóbal, J. (2018). Complexity and project management: A general overview. *Complexity, 2018.* https://doi.org/10.1155/2018/

4891286

Castillo-Montoya, M. (2016). Preparing for interview research: The interview protocol refinement framework. *The Qualitative Report, 21*(5), 811–831. https://doi.org/10.46743/2160-3715/2016.2337

Chang, T., Deng, X., Hwang, B., & Zhao, X. (2018). Identifying political risk management strategies in international construction projects. *Advances in Civil Engineering.* https://doi.org/10.1155/2018/1016384

Charkhakan, M., & Heravi, G. (2019). Evaluating the preventability of conflicts arising from change occurrence in construction projects. *Engineering, Construction, and Architectural Management, 26*(8), 1777–1800. https://doi.org/10.1108/ECAM-09-2018-0361

Chileshe, N., & Kavishe, N. (2018). Identifying project management practices and principles for public-private partnerships in housing projects: The case of Tanzania. *Sustainability, 10*(12), 4609. https://doi.org/10.3390/su10124609

Chong, S., & Herath, S. (2021). Key components and critical success factors for project management success: A literature review. *Operations and Supply Chain Management: An International Journal, 14*(4), 431–443. https://doi.org/10.31387/oscm0470314

Ciric, D., Delic, M., Gracanin, D., Lalic, B., Medic, N., & Tasic, N. (2019). Agile vs. traditional approach in project management: Strategies, challenges, and reasons to introduce agile. *Procedia Manufacturing, 39*, 1407–1414. https://doi.org/10.1016/j.promfg.2020.01.314

Clark, K. R., & Vealé, B. L. (2018). Strategies to enhance data collection and analysis in qualitative research. *Radiologic Technology, 89*(5), 482CT–485CT.

Cook, K., Gray, L., Rempel, G., & Wong-Wylie, G. (2020). Expanding qualitative research interviewing strategies: Zoom video communications. *The Qualitative Report, 25*(5), 1292–1301.

Corti, B., Golini, R., & Landoni, P. (2017). More efficient project execution and evaluation with logical framework and project cycle management: evidence from international development projects. *Impact Assessment and Project Appraisal,* 35:2, 128–138, https://doi.org/10.1080/14615517.2016.123 9495

Cox, J. F., III. (2021). Using the theory of constraints' processes of ongoing improvement to address the provider appointment scheduling system execution problem. *Health Systems, 10*(1), 41–72. https://doi.org/10.1080/20476965.201 9.1646105

Cox, J. F., & Boyd, L. H. (2020). Using the theory of constraints' processes of ongoing improvement to address the provider appointment scheduling design problem. *Health Systems, 9*(2), 124–158. https://doi.org/10.1080/20476965.2 018.1471439

Cox, J., & Schleier, J. (2010). *Theory of constraints handbook.* McGraw-Hill.

Creasy, T., Fan, Y., & Johnson, N. (2016). Recent trends in theory use and application within project management discipline. *Journal of Engineering, Project, and Production Management, 6*(1), 25–52. http://www.ppml.url.tw/EPPM_Journal/volumns/06 _01_January_2016/ID_128_06_01_25_52.pdf

Creswell, J. W. (2005). *Educational research: Planning, conducting, and evaluating quantitative and qualitative research.* Merrill.

Cristovão, L., Gaspar, M., & Tenera, A. (2019). Theory of constraints thinking processes on operational lean programs management improvement: An energy producer company case. In *Doctoral Conference on Computing, Electrical and Industrial Systems,* 125–142. Springer.

Dalei, N., Garg, S., Sunder, R., & Upreti, N. (2019). Application of theory of constraints to foster the services of Indian power transmission system. *International Journal of Energy and Sector Management, 14*(3). 547–568. https://doi.org/10.1108/IJESM-05-2019-0007

Damoah, I. S., Akwei, C. A., Amoako, I. O., & Botchie, D. (2018). Corruption as a source of government project failure in developing countries: Evidence from Ghana. *Project Management Journal, 49*(3), 1733. https://doi.org/10.1177/8756972818770587

Dan-asabe, B., Unegbu, H., & Yawas, D. (2020). An investigation of the relationship between project performance measures and project management practices of construction projects for the construction industry in Nigeria. *Journal of King Saud University-Engineering Science.* https://doi.org/10.1016/j.jksues.2020.10.001

de Carvalho, M, & Santos, P. (2021). Exploring the challenges and benefits for scaling agile project management to large projects: A review. *Requirements Engineering, 27,* 117–134. https://doi.org/10.1007/s00766-021-00363-3

DeJonckheere, M., & Vaughn, L. M. (2019). Semistructured interviewing in primary care research: a balance of relationship and rigour. *Family medicine and community health, 7*(2), e000057. https://doi.org/10.1136/fmch-2018-000057

Díaz-Barcos, V., Lozano, S., Ortiz-Marcos, I., & Rodríguez-Rivero, R. (2020). Applying the strategic prospective approach to project management in a development project in Columbia. *International Journal of Project Management, 38*(8), 534–547.

https://doi.org/10.1016/j.ijproman.2020.07.003

Dohl, S., Lee, Z., & Rahman, R. (2021). Critical success factors for implementing design-build: Analyzing Malaysian public projects. *Journal of Engineering, Design, and Technology, Vol, ahead-of-print No. ahead-of-print.* https://doi.org/10.1108/JEDT-08-2020-0321

Donnelly, J., & Ika, L. (2017). Success conditions for international development capacity building projects. *International Journal of Project Management, 35,* 44–63. https://doi.org/10.1016/j.ijproman.2016.10.005

Dostatni, E., & Trojanowska, J. (2017). Application of the theory of constraint for project management. *Management and Production Engineering Review, 8*(3), 87–95. https://doi.org/10.1515/mper-2017-0031

Ebrahimzadeh, S., Karimi, R., McCarthy, D., Mojtahedi, M., Sepasgozar, S., & Shirowzhan, S. (2019). Delay causes and emerging digital tools: A novel model of delay analysis, including integrated project delivery and PMBOK. *Buildings, 9*(9), 191. https://doi.org/10.3390/buildings9090191

Ellis, T., & Levy, Y. (2009). Towards a guide for novice researchers on research methodology: Review and proposed methods. *Issues in Informing Science and Information Technology 6,* 323–337. http://www.informingscience.org/journals/iisit/overview

Elshwadfy, L., & Ibrahim, A. (2021). Factors affecting the accuracy of construction project cost estimation in Egypt. *Jordan Journal of Civil Engineering, 15*(3), 329–344. https://www.researchgate.net/publication/353147794_Factors_Affecting_the_Accuracy_of_Construction_Project_Cost_Estimation_in_Egypt

Evans, C., & Lewis, J. (2018). Analyzing semistructured

interviews using thematic analysis: exploring voluntary civil participation among adults. SAGE Publications Ltd. https://dx.doi.org/10.4135/9781526439284

Eweje, G., Latif, K., Sajjad, A., & Shaukat, M. (2021). Revisiting the relationship between sustainable project management and project success: The moderating role of stakeholder engagement and team building. *Sustainable Development, 30*(1), 58–75. https://doi.org/10.1002/sd.2228

Feldman, S., & Shaw, L. (2019). The epistemological and ethical challenges of archiving and sharing qualitative data. *American Behavioral Scientist, 63*(6), 699–721. https://doi.org/10.1177/0002764218796084

Fernandes, G., Ferreira, M., Loureiro, I., Ribeiro, P., & Tereso, A. (2019). Project management practices in private organizations. *Project Management Journal, 50*(1), 6–22. https://doi.org/10.1177/8756972818810966

Flick, U. (2018). *Triangulation in data collection. The sage handbook of qualitative data collection* (pp. 527–544). *SAGE Publications Ltd.* https://uk.sagepub.com/en-gb/eur/the-sage-handbook-of-qualitative-data-collection/book249900#contents

Fusch, G. E., Fusch, P., & Ness, L. R. (2018). Denzin's Paradigm Shift: Revisiting Triangulation in Qualitative Research. *Journal of Social Change, 10*(1), 19–32, https://doi.org/10.5590/JOSC.2018.10.1.02

Ganguly, K. (2019). Establishing a link between quality management and supply chain risk management, a fuzzy AHP approach. *The TQM Journal,* 1754–2731. https://doi.org/10.1108/TQM-05-2019-0125

Ghaljaie, F., Goli, H., & Naderifar, M. (2017). Snowball Sampling: A purposeful method of sampling in qualitative research. *Strides in Development of Medical Education, 14*(3), https://doi.org/10.5812/sdme.67670

Goldratt, E. (1999). *Theory of constraints*. North River Press, Great.

Golini, R., Kalchschmidt, M., & Landoni, P. (2018). The adoption of the logical framework in international development projects: A survey of non-governmental organizations. *Impact Assessment and Project Appraisal, 36*(2), 145–154. https://doi.org/10.1080/14615517.2017.1354643

Golmohammadi, D. (2015). A study of scheduling under the theory of constraints. *International Journal of Production Economics, 135*, 38–50. https://doi.org/10.1016/j.ijpe.2015.03.015

Golmohammadi, D., & Mansouri, S. A. (2015). Complexity and workload considerations in product mix decisions under the theory of constraints. *Naval Research Logistics, 62*(5), 357–369. https://doi.org/10.1002/nav.21632

Grida, M., & Zeid, M. (2019). A system dynamics-based model to implement the theory of constraints in a healthcare system. *Simulation: Transactions of the Society for Modeling and Simulation International, 95*(7), 593–605. https://doi.org/10.1177/0037549718788953

Gunduz, M., & Almuajebh, M. (2020). Critical success factors for sustainable construction project management. *Sustainability, 12*(5). Article 1990. https://doi.org/10.3390/su12051990

Gustafsson, J. (2017). Single case studies vs. multiple case studies: A comparative study. Academy of Business, Engineering and Science Halmstad University. http://www.diva-portal.org/smash/get/diva2:1064378/FULLTEXT01.pdf

Haaskjold, H., Andersen, B., Laedre, O., & Aarseth, W. (2019). Factors affecting transaction costs and collaboration in projects. *International Journal of Managing Projects in Business, 13*(1), 197230. https://doi.org/10.1108/IJMPB-09-2018-0197

Haque, A., Kumar, A., Kumar, L., Kumari, M., Mangutkar, S., & Verma, M. (2021). Study on greening project management practices for sustainable construction: A review. *Journal of Emerging Technologies and Innovative Research, 8*(4), 708–715. https://www.researchgate.net/publication/353917485_Study_on_greening_project_management_practices_for_sustainable_construction

Hancock, D. R., & Algozzine, B. (2017). *Doing case study research: A practical guide for beginning researchers* (3rd ed.). Teachers College Press.

Harmony (2016). What is strategy & tactic trees? Harmony. https://www.harmonytoc.com/what-is-toc-strategy-and-tactic-trees [Accessed 16th, August 2020]

Hasan, R., Sato, C., & Tinoco, R. (2016). Responsible project management: Beyond the triple constraints. *The Journal of Modern Project Management, 4*(1), 80–93. https://www.journalmodernpm.com/index.php/jmpm/article/view/179

Holweg, M., & Maylor, H. (2018). Lean leadership in major projects: from predict and provide to predict and prevent. *International Journal of Operations and Production Management, 38*(6), 1368–1386. https://doi.org/10.1108/IJOPM-02-2017-0100

Ika, L., Landoni, P., Munro, L., & Söderlund, J. (2020). Cross-learning between project management and international development: Analysis and research agenda. *International Journal of Project Management, 38*(8), 548–558. https://doi.org/10.1016/j.ijproman.2020.10.005

Ika, L., Landoni, P., Munro, L., & Söderlund, J. (2020). When project management meets international development, what can we learn. *International Journal of Project Management, 38*(8), 469–473. https://doi.org/10.1016/j.ijproman.2020.10.004

Ika, L., & Munro, L. (2020). Guided by the beauty of our weapons: Comparing project management standards inside and outside international development. *Development in Practice, 30*(7), 934–952. https://doi.org/10.1080/09614524.2020.176 6421

Isharyanto, F., Parker, W. D., & Parsons, N. (2015). Inclusion of strategic management theories to project management. *International Journal of Managing Projects in Business, 8*(3), 552–573. https://doi.org/10.1108/IJMPB-11-2014-0079

Izmailov, A., Korneva, D., & Kozhemiakin, A. (2016). Effective project management with theory of constraints. *Procedua - Social and Behavioral Sciences, 229*, 96–103. https://doi.org/ 10.1016/j.sbspro.2016.07.118

Johnson, C. W., & Rose, J. (2020). Contextualizing reliability and validity in qualitative research: Toward more rigorous and trustworthy qualitative social science in leisure research. *Journal of Leisure Research, 51*(4), 432–451. https://doi.org/ 10.1080/00222216.2020.1722042

Jokkaw, N., & Tongthong, T. (2017). Measurement of the importance of knowledge areas and competency levels of construction project managers in the Lao PDR. *Engineering and Applied Science Research, 44*(1), 20–26. https://doi.org/ 10.14456/easr.2017.3

Jugend, D., Luiz, J., Luiz, O., Salgado, M., da Silva, S., & de Souza, F. (2019). Impact of critical chain project management and product portfolio management on new product development performance. *Journal of Business & Industrial Marketing, 34*(8), 1692–1705. https://www.researchgate.net/publication/

335369631_Impact_of_critical_chain_project_management_and_product_portfolio_management_on_new_product_development_performance

Jugend, D., Luiz, J., Luiz, O., & de Souza, F. (2018). Linking the critical chain project management literature. *International Journal of Managing Projects in Business, 12*(2), 423–443. https://www.proquest.com/docview/2239132736

Kaijun, L., Lin, P., Wen, S., & Xuejun, H. (2017). Schedule of supply chain management project based on TOC. *Journal of Intelligent & Fuzzy Systems, 33*, 2801–2809. https://doi.org/10.3233/JIFS-169329

Kamu, F., & Paul, S. (2018). Effect of project management practices on performance of construction projects in Laikipia County, Kenya. *International Journal of Recent Research in Social Sciences and Humanities, 5*(2), 7–13.

Korstjens, I., & Moser, A. (2017). Series: Practical guidance to qualitative research. Part 2: Context, research questions and designs. *European Journal of General Practice, 23*(1), 274–279. https://doi.org/10.1080/13814788.2017.1375090

Kozhakhmetova, A., Zhidebekkyzy, A., Turginbayeva, A., & Akhmetova, Z., (2019). Modelling of project success factors: A cross-cultural comparison. *Economics & Sociology, 12*(2), 219–234. https://doi.org/10.14254/2071-789X.2019/12-2/13

Lacerda, T., Librelato, P., Rodrigues, H., & Veit, R. (2014). A process improvement approach based on the value stream mapping and the theory of constraints thinking process. *Business Process Management Journal, 20*(6), 922–949. https://doi.org/10.1108/BPMJ-07-2013-0098

Laishram, B., & Thounaojam, N. (2021). Issues in promoting sustainability in mega infrastructure projects: A systematic review. *Journal of Environmental Planning and Management,* 1–24. https://doi.org/10.1080/09640568.2021.1941810

Leung, L. (2015). Validity, reliability, and generalizability in qualitative research. *Journal of Family Medicine and Primary Care, 4*(3), 324–327. https://doi.org/10.4103/2249-4863.161306

Li, Y., Shou, Y., Sun, H., & Sun, T. (2020). What makes a competent international project manager in emerging and developing countries? *Project Management Journal 51*(2), 181–198. https://doi.org/10.1177/8756972820901387

Liljedahl, M., McGrath, C., & Palmgren, P. (2019). Twelve tips for conducting qualitative research interviews. *Medical Teacher, 41*(9), 1002–1006. https://doi.org/10.1080/0142159X.2018.1497149

Mabin, V., & Mirzaei, M. (2017). Agile project management and public policy development projects: a case study of New Zealand. *New Zealand Journal of Applied Business Research (NZJABR), 15*(1), 59–75. https://www.researchgate.net/publication/321145063_Agile_Project_Management_and_Public_c_Policy_Development_Projects_A_case_study_from_New_Zealand

Madill, A., & Sullivan, P. (2018). Mirrors, portraits, and member checking: Managing difficult moments of knowledge exchange in the social sciences. *Qualitative Psychology, 5*(3), 321. https://doi.org/10.1037/qup0000089

Mainga, W. (2017). Examining project learning, project management competencies, and project efficiency in project-based firms (PBFs). *International Journal of Managing Projects in Business, 10*(2), 454–504. https://doi.org/10.1108/IJMPB-04-2016-0035

March, S., Müller, B., & Niederman, F. (2018). Using process theory for accumulating project management knowledge: A seven-category model. *Project Management Journal, 49*(1), 6–24. https://doi.org/10.1177/8756972281804900102

Martinsuo, M. (2020). The management of values in project business: Adjusting beliefs to transform project practices and outcomes. *Project Management Journal, 51*(4), 389–399. https://doi.org/10.1177/8756972820927890

Melendez, J. R., Zoghbe Nunez, Y. A., Malvacias Escalona, A. M., Almeida, G. A, & Layana Ruiz, J. (2018). Theory of constraints: A systematic review from the management context. *Revista Espacios, 39*(48). https://www.revistaespacios.com/a18v39n48/a18v39n48p01.pdf

Messner, W. (2015). Measuring existent intercultural effectiveness in global teams. *International Journal of Managing Projects in Business, 8*(1), 107–132. https://doi.org/10.1108/IJMPB-05-2014-0044

Mihić, M., Miković, R., Obradović, V., Petrović, D., & Todorović, M. (2020). The integration of social capital and knowledge management: The key challenge for international development and cooperation projects of nonprofit organizations. *International Journal of Project Management, 38*(8), 515–533. https://doi.org/10.1016/j.ijproman.2020.07.006

Mishra, P. K. (2016). Managing international development projects: Case studies of implementation of large-scale projects in India, *International Journal of Rural Management, 12*(I), 4–26. https://doi.org/10.1177/0973005216633955

McMullen, T. (1998). *Introduction to the theory of constraints (TOC) management system.* APICS.

Molenaar, K., Ortiz, J., & Pellicer, E. (2019). Determining contingencies in the management of construction projects. *Project Management Journal, 50*(2), 226–242. https://doi.org/

10.1177/8756972819827389

National Commission for the Protection of Human Subjects and Biomedical and Behavioral Research (1979). *The Belmont Report: Ethical principles and guidelines for the protection of human subjects of research.* U.S. Department of Health and Human Services. https://www.hhs.gov/ohrp/humansubjects/guidance/Belmont.html

Nevstad, K., Madsen, T. K., Eskerod, P., Aarseth, W. K., Karlsen, A. S. T., & Andersen, B. (2021). Linking partnering success factors to project performance: Findings from two nationwide surveys. *Project Leadership and Society, 2,* Article 100009. https://doi.org/10.1016/j.plas.2021.100009

Ngala, M., Obwatho, S., & Owuori, P. (2020). Project management practices, corporate governance and sustainability: A critical literature review. *Journal of Human Resource & Leadership, 4*(2), 30–47. Retrieved from https://stratfordjournals.org/journals/index.php/journal-of-human-resource/article/view/506

Park, J. E. (2021). Schedule delays of major projects: What should we do about it?. *Transport Reviews, 41*(6), 814–832. https://doi.org/10.1080/01441647.2021.1915897

Paulmakesh, A., & Yimer, Y. (2021). Implementation of project management for strategy realisation. *Journal of University Shanghai for Science and Technology, 23*(10), 887–892. https://jusst.org/wp-content/uploads/2021/10/Implementation-Of-Project-Management-For-Strategy-Realisation.pdf

Picciotto, R. (2020). Towards a new project management movement? An international development perspective. *International of Journal of Project Management, 38*(8), 474–485. https://doi.org/10.1016.j.ijproman.2019.08.002

Pirju, I. (2018). The importance on communication in

project management strategy. *Acta Universitatis Danubius, 12*(2), 152–161. https://sta.uwi.edu/eng/wije/vol4002_jan2018/documents/Abs0618012v40n2p4250VRagbirJan1801.pdf

Pollack, J., Helm, J., & Adler, D. (2018). What is the iron triangle, and how has it changed? *International Journal of Managing Projects in Business, 11*(2), 527547. https://doi.org/10.1108/IJMPB-09-2017-0107

Pretorius, J. H. C., Pretorius, L., & Van Wyngaard, C. J. (2012). Theory of the triple constraint – A conceptual review. *2012 IEEE International Conference on Industrial Engineering and Engineering Management, Industrial Engineering and Engineering Management (IEEM), 2012 IEEE International Conference on,* 1991. https://doi.org/10.1109/IEEM.2012.6838095

Project Management Institute. (2017). *A guide to the project management body of knowledge: PMBOK guide* (6th ed.).

Project Managment Institute. (2022). *Global megatrends 2022.*

Punb, K., & Ragbir, V. (2018). Customising a project management framework at a Trinidad-based paper manufacturer: A case study. *West Indian Journal of Engineering, 40*(2), 42–51.

Quigley, C. F., & Simpson, A. (2016). Member checking process with adolescent students: Not just reading a transcript. *The Qualitative Report, 21*(2), 376–392. https://nsuworks.nova.edu/tqr/vol21/iss2/12

Roberts, L. (2015). Ethical issues in conducting qualitative research in online communities. *Qualitative Research in Psychology, 12*(3), 314–325.

Sapiuly, K. (2017). Project management as a tool to implement the strategy, the realities, and prospects of oil and gas enterprises in the Republic of Kazakhstan. *Proceedings of the Voronezh State University of Engineering Technologies, 79*(1),

332–337. https://doi.org/10.20914/2310-1202-2017-1-332-337

Saunders, M. N. K., Lewis, P., & Thornhill, A. (2015). *Research methods for business students* (7th ed.). Pearson Education Limited.

Soltani, R., & Zohrehvandi, S. (2022). Project scheduling and buffer management: A comprehensive review and future directions. *Journal of Project Management, 7*(2), 121–132. https://doi.org/10.5267/j.jpm.2021.9.002

Spiers, J., Morse, J. M., Olson, K., Mayan, M., & Barrett, M. (2018). Reflection/Commentary on a Past Article: "Verification strategies for establishing reliability and validity in qualitative research." *International Journal of Qualitative Methods, 17*. https://doi.org/10.1177/1609406918788237

Stratton, R., & Yeong, A. (2017). Capturing action research knowledge through strategy and tactic tree. In: EurOMA 2017: 24th International Conference the European Operations Management Association, Heriot-Watt University, 1–5 July 2017.

Techt, U. (2014). *Goldratt and the Theory of Constraints: The Quantum Leap in Management.* Columbia University Press.

Thompson, R. (2018). A qualitative phenomenological study of emotional and cultural intelligence of international students in the United States of America. *Journal of International Student, 8*(2), 1220–1255. https://doi.org/10.5281/zenodo.1250423

Trochim, W. (2020). Research Methods Knowledge Basc. Conjoint.ly. https://conjointly.com/kb/qualitative-validity/

Urban, W. (2019). TOC implementation in a medium-scale manufacturing system with diverse product rooting. *Production & Manufacturing Researc, 7*(1), 178–194. https://doi.org/10.1080/21693277.2019.1616002

Vereijssen, J., Srinivasan, M. S., Dirks, S., Fielke, S., Jongmans, C., Agnew, N., Klerkx, L., Pinxterhuis, I., Moore, J., Edwards, P., Brazendale, R., Botha, N., & Turner, J. A. (2017). Addressing complex challenges using a co-innovation approach: lessons from five case studies in the New Zealand primary sector. *Outlook on Agriculture, 46*(2), 108116. https://doi.org/10.1177/0030727017712321

Vignesh, T., & Vijayabanu, C. (2018). Critical factors determining the success of the public-private partnership in construction projects: An Indian context. *Journal of Modern Project Management,* 24–39. https://doi.org/10.19255/JMPM01503

Vijaykar, S. (2021). Conflict resolution in a multi-level IT-enabled outsourcing network: A structured solution approach. *Journal of International Technology and Information Management, 30*(1), 134–169. https://scholarworks.lib.csusb.edu/jitim/vol30/iss1/5

Walden University. (2021). Doctoral study rubric and research handbook. Available from http://academicguides.waldenu.edu/researchcenter/osra/dba

Wang, X., & Zhou, Z. (2022). Discussions on project management and its success: A comprehensive theoretical review. *Scientific and Social Research 4.2 (2022),* 30–35.

Watt, D. (2007). On becoming a qualitative researcher: The value of reflexivity. *The Qualitative Report, 12*(1), 82–101. http://www.nova.edu/ssss/QR-12-1/watt.pdf

Yap, J. B. H., Abdul-Rahman, H., & Chen, W. (2017). Collaborative model: Managing design changes with reusable project experiences through project learning and effective communication. *International Journal of Project Management, 35*(7), 12531271. https://doi.org/10.1016/j.ijproman.2017.04.

010

Yap, J. B. H., Abdul-Rahman, H., & Wang, C. (2018). Preventive mitigation of overruns with project communication management and continuous learning: PLS-SEM approach. *Journal of Construction Engineering and Management, 144*(5), Article 04018025. https://doi.org/10.1061/(ASCE)CO.1943-7862.0001456

Yin, R. (2015). *Qualitative research from start to finish, Second Edition.* The Guilford Press.

Yin, R. (2018). *Case study research and applications: Design and methods, Sixth Edition.* Sage.

34

Appendix: Interview Protocol

My Actions
Script
Preparation:

I will contact the PMI UAE Chapter leaders to obtain approval to distribute my study participant request to prepare the interviews. Once I receive the list of participants, I will send out informed consent forms. Another exchange and introduction will occur to answer any questions the participants may have, and then I will schedule the interview. I will explain the purpose of the study, their right to withdraw, and their confidentiality. I also discuss that there are no incentives for participating and their role in the research.

Introduction of the interview.

Hello, thank you for participating in my doctoral study interview. I appreciate your time today. Shall we get started?

- Watch for non-verbal queues
- Paraphrase as needed

- Ask follow-up probing questions
- to get more in-depth

1. What strategies are you using to identify and address your organization's international development projects' triple constraints?
2. What method(s) did you find worked best to motivate your stakeholders to communicate and address international development projects' triple constraints with each other?
3. How have you found success in meeting the triple constraints of your past international development projects?
4. How are you finding success in meeting the triple constraints of your current international development projects?
5. How, if at all, has the theory of constraints assisted you in your international development projects' success?

Follow-Up

1. Based upon your organization's experience, what were the primary causes of your international development projects' failing to meet their quality-related goals?
2. Based upon your organization's experiences, what were the primary causes of our international development projects' exceeding their budgets?
3. Based on your organization's experiences, what were the primary causes of your international development projects' delays?
4. What else can you share with me about your organization's strategies and processes to successfully address international development projects' triple constraints?

Wrap up interview thanking participant.

Thank you so much for answering all of the questions to the best of your knowledge. You have given profound feedback for my study. Are there any questions you may have for me?

Schedule follow-up member checking interview.

I would like to schedule a follow-up interview to interpret the synthesis of the answers you have given. When is a good time for you?

Follow-up Member Checking Interview

- Review and interpret the interview transcripts
- Write synthesis after each question
- Provide a printed or digital copy of the synthesis to the participant
- Ask the participant if the synthesis is aligned with the answers given or if there is
- additional information to add
- Continue member checking until data is fulfilled

Follow-up interview introduction.

Hello, thank you once again for your time today. Today we will complete a follow-up interview based on the feedback you received regarding your interview answers' synthesis. Shall we get started?

Concise synthesis of each interview question. Script to include "what would you like to add?"